EASTWARD

EASTWARD

A Maine Cruise
in a Friendship Sloop

by Roger F. Duncan

Originally published in 1976 by
International Marine Publishing.

ISBN: 0-942396-73-1

Cover Painting by Earle G. Barlow
Maps by Deena Stearns

Blackberry Books
617 East Neck Road
Nobleboro, Maine   04555

Gulf of Maine Bioregion

THIS BOOK IS DEDICATED TO THE MEMORY OF MY FATHER, ROBERT FULLER DUNCAN.

CONTENTS

PREFACE

There are two kinds of people: indoor people and outdoor people. Each makes his contribution, but this book is written for outdoor people, for the skiers, the mountaineers, the surfers, the sailors.

Writing is like looking through binoculars. You must select from the whole horizon what you want to look at. Then in a narrow field of view you see enlarged and clarified a single object. Your attention is for the moment concentrated on that one bird or peak or distant island. Through this book I would help you to see through my binoculars and by sharing mine, to sharpen the focus on your own.

This book is the product of many people's effort. I have acknowledged in its pages the contributions of Murray Peterson and James Chadwick, designer and builder of *Eastward*, and the contributions of those who helped us fit out and get off. I must also thank my crews: Donald and Nancy Duncan, Mr. and Mrs. Gerald Birks, Harold Prenatt, and Robert Duncan. Mrs. Howard Taylor typed most of the manuscript and contributed many useful suggestions. Hugh G. Williams helped with the difficult job of getting the book started and contributed honest and useful criticism. Especially I want to thank my wife, Mary, first mate and foredeck hand, one of the few ladies who can and will take in a gaff topsail in a breeze of wind.

Roger F. Duncan
East Boothbay, Maine

EASTWARD

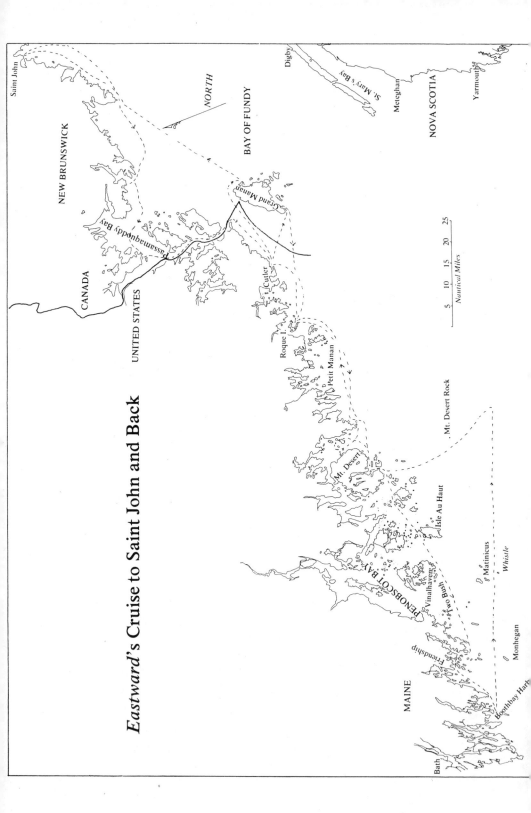

Eastward's Cruise to Saint John and Back

1 Cruising—An Introduction

We sailed gently northeastward along the shore of North Haven Island in Penobscot Bay before a gentle westerly on the best of Maine mornings. The Camden Hills were blue to port, the shore of North Haven a variety of grays and greens to starboard. We trailed a fishline, occasionally catching a mackerel — loveliest of fish. The day was young, warm and bright.

Under Webster Head lay a yacht at anchor. An outboard put off from her side and rushed out at us, its pilot waving. A cherished friend and veteran cruising man, really a very pleasant person despite his violent approach, tied alongside, drank a bottle of beer, and left us with this solemn advice:

To have a good vacation — Never Beat

In the literal sense he was wrong, for a stout beat to windward can be good for body, mind, and soul; but in a figurative sense he was right. On a cruise, the successful man is one who does not pit himself against wind, weather and time. Much less concerned with where he goes than with how he gets there and what he does when he arrives, the wise cruising man makes the most of the weather and the coast, seeking ever to find something to enjoy and remember.

Almost everyone knows this, but so few people pay any attention to it. How seldom do we see a sailing yacht becalmed? How seldom do we see anyone beating down Muscle Ridge Channel, or sailing into a harbor, or stopping to jig up a codfish? How often do we see the elegant yacht, all sails furled, motoring through early morning calm and gentle morning airs in order to "get somewhere"?

This book is the celebration of a cruise. From its table of contents and track charts, it appears to be the account of a cruise from East Boothbay, Maine, to Saint John, New Brunswick, and back; but it is more than an account of ports visited and weather encountered. It tells how we feel about what happened to us, for these feelings are what make a cruise memorable long after the snapshots are dog-eared and faded. Because feelings are accumulated from past experience, the book abounds in reminiscences of other cruises, personal reflections, tales of other men's exploits, and digressions into history and literature. May this book add a dimension to your next adventure on salt water.

The author with a fair wind to the eastward.

The mate at the wheel. It can get cold offshore, even in the summer.

2 A Mad Start

The cruise started on a wrong note, a note of exurban frustration with time, weather, and geography. Fresh from the pressure of the loose ends of the academic year, we hurled ourselves into the pressure of preparation for sea with the same sense of desperate haste.

Our first mistake was to set a firm date for departure. We were determined to sail on July first for Yarmouth, Nova Scotia, there to take aboard Mr. and Mrs. Birks. This date stood before us like another of the deadlines we had been fighting to meet all year. When on June twenty-first we arrived at our home on the shore of Linekin Bay in the dusk of a foggy afternoon, we knew that we were in for another battle.

From the wharf at Reed's yard in Boothbay Harbor we looked at *Eastward* next morning, her bottom and topsides freshly painted, rolling high in the water, mastless, engineless, and bare. We went aboard and found the deck nasty with the accumulated droppings of gulls and foul with crab shells and sea urchin carcasses, gummy and stinking in the fog. At least we could clean her off! That done, we looked ahead to July first and saw our trim, neat Friendship sloop, deck and spars shining in new paint, mast stepped, rigging set up, sails bent and engine functional. In our mind's eye she sat trim in the water, her cruising gear aboard, cabin neat, sleeping bags and duffel bags stowed. With her ensign snapping in a fair, warm southerly breeze, we saw ourselves cast off, head eastward out to sea, and tear July first off the calendar.

It didn't work out that way. The Management accumulated a huge volume of warm, moist air over the Atlantic Ocean and arranged for it to flow steadily northwestward into New England. As it passed over our cold coastal waters, its moisture condensed into heavy, wet fog, broken occasionally by gleams of muggy sunshine and heavy tropical showers. For two solid weeks the fog was to persist.

Nevertheless, with eyes firmly fixed on our picture of July first, we went to work. We brought into our shop everything we could move — gaff, staysail boom, blocks, wire rigging, engine parts. We sanded, cleaned, painted, repaired, and greased. When the sun broke through, we went outside and sanded mast and boom, painting between showers.

Utterly frustrated by an afternoon of heavy rain, we gave up work and drove to Sargentville to pick up our new topsail from Clarence Hale, our sailmaker. It was a pleasant, if damp, interlude; but we came home to Linekin Bay and turned in to the persistent notes of the horns on three lighthouses.

We installed and bolted down the engine in fog and drizzle, hooked up carburetor, starter, distributor, generator, and fuel pump. We wired her up, tried her out, and she balked. Still, we had to get on with it, so we loaded all the rigging into our Scout, trucked it to the yard and hung it on the mast as it lay on two horses on the wharf. We moved rapidly here, but not hastily, checking carefully each shroud and stay to be sure it was sound and was properly led. Every hook and shackle pin we moused with marline. Every cotter pin we spread and taped. Every turnbuckle we wiped with hard grease. Surely the next day would give us a break in the weather. July first was almost upon us.

On June 30th there was no break. In continued fog and drizzle we towed *Eastward* to the wharf, stepped the mast, and spent the rest of a long day sorting out rigging, setting up lanyards, and bending sails. On the night before our scheduled departure we sailed from boatyard

wharf to nearby mooring in the misty dusk, *Eastward* at last moving
under her own power. But it was clearly impossible to leave the next
day; we had failed to achieve our goal.

Breathlessly working long hours every day, we hurried on. The
engine responded at last on July second. We launched our float at
Linekin Bay on July third and planned to bring *Eastward* over from
Boothbay Harbor to load cruising gear. But on that day the depthfinder ceased to function. The electronics expert gave us a gloomy
prognosis, and I did not want to sail without the instrument. Know-
ing that on July Fourth we could get no help from electronics expert
or boatyard and that the ensuing weekend would then pass and find
us still in Boothbay Harbor, I incontinently bought a new depthfinder
and persuaded the yard to haul us, install the transducer, and launch
us again on the same tide. Late that afternoon we motored out of
hot and muggy Boothbay into a solid bank of fog. We emerged in
front of our own float, tired, dirty, frustrated, and three days late
already.

At supper it occurred to us that on July Fourth all grocery stores
would be closed. We hurried uptown and raided the supermarket,
picking up whatever looked as though it would be useful, too tired
to think. We picked our way through the press of leisurely vacation-
ists buying coke, potato chips, and watermelons, looking for corned
beef, canned stew, pilot crackers, and beans. We loaded two carts
and nearly fell asleep standing in line.

On the Fourth the drift of warm and gentle air continued, still con-
densing as it came. We could not see the mile across Linekin Bay as
we put cruising gear aboard. We knew it was unwise to put damp
bunk cushions on damp bunks, to put aboard charts and books limp
with fog. The iron Shipmate stove, unblacked, showed tiny red spots
of rust where the fog dew struck it. Sleeping bags, duffel bags, food,
briquets, life preservers, emergency raft, anchor line, and tools we
lugged aboard, damp or dripping. We knew it was foolish. We knew
it was desperate; but if we were ever to go to Yarmouth, Nova Scotia,
we had to start and this was the day to do it.

Even our casting off was hasty and anti-climatic, for our mainsail, once hoisted, had to be lowered again to clear a tangle in the topsail gear.

At last, at three o'clock in the afternoon, heavily loaded, hastily prepared, desperately hurried, we dropped our dock lines, set jib and staysail, and swung off into the fog for Yarmouth, Nova Scotia.

Eastward. *The bag on the end of the bowsprit holds the jib topsail.*

3 Eastward and Her Crew

What manner of people are we who act in such fashion? We spend most of the year in school. I am a teacher and assistant headmaster; my wife Mary is a tutor for elementary students with special needs. My brother Donald is a teacher of mathematics and head of his department. His daughter Nancy, fifteen, is a student and an amateur actress. We are not intrepid mariners of outstanding courage and endurance, voyaging impossible Pacific seas in search of the unattainable, euphoric tropic isles. We are summer sailors, having cruised the Maine coast for many seasons, accustomed to fog, to hard and puffy northwesters, to smoky southwesters, to squall and calm. We know the loom of spruce-clad granite in a fog, the profile of Isle au Haut and the tall, slim shaft of Petit Manan Light. We have rolled at anchor in Monhegan Harbor, fought mosquitoes at Cape Small, and admired the sunset over Englishman Bay from Roque Island. We have dug clams at Trafton's Island, jigged codfish off Roaring Bull, and eaten smoked herring on Grand Manan.

We have accomplished no great feats of valor at sea, but each year we try to find a new harbor, we seek out a new experience, we try to go a little beyond what we have done before. This year the goal is the eastern shore of the Bay of Fundy.

Together we have sailed in *Eastward* before. She is a Friendship sloop, thirty-two feet long, rigged as her picture shows with main and jib topsails. Designed by Murray Peterson and built in 1956 to sail parties, she has a large cockpit to accommodate six passengers comfortably. She is dry, stiff, and built to sail on her bottom. When she does lean over to it, people don't feel as if they were about to fall off her. She is a workboat type, like those developed for fishing and lobstering on the Maine coast in the early years of the century. Her workboat characteristics make her dry, fast, comfortable and handy.

Below, she has four bunks and a galley with a Shipmate stove that burns coal, wood, briquets, or almost anything flammable. There is also an alcohol stove for quick heat. Her cabin is simply and even roughly fitted out, for we did all the carpentry ourselves, figuring that if we did not like the plan, we could tear it out with a wrecking bar in half an hour and start again. We liked it, so we painted it gray and white and left it.

She has a four-cylinder gasoline engine that lives under the cockpit floor. Despite days and even weeks of neglect, once properly adjusted, the machine is amazingly good-tempered and responds enthusiastically.

Her rigging is heavy and on the "safe" side, everything being two sizes larger than is really necessary. Boatyards laugh at us for using three-eighth-inch stainless steel shrouds. You could lift her out of water with one of them. The anchors are thirty-five and seventy-five pounders, the anchor line three-quarter-inch nylon with three fathoms of five-sixteenth-inch chain on the small one and three-eighth-inch chain on the big one. As one fisherman observed, "It would ride her to bottom." Running rigging, spars, and sails are all unduly heavy, but the rig is in no sense a short rig. Murray Peterson knew enough about Maine in the summer to know that a successful boat must be disgracefully over-canvassed by ordinary standards. Should it come on to blow, she can be reefed.

A radio direction finder and a depth sounder are the extent of our electronic gear. The former is interesting and often helpful, but the depth sounder is without doubt one of the most valuable inventions of the century. Over and over again we have used it to correct our dead-reckoning errors in the fog or at night. Next to compass and clock, it is the most useful tool aboard.

She is, in short, a great boat — fun to sail, easy to handle and capable in difficult going. With the stove hot and the lamps lit, she is a pleasant place to be at the end of a long day.

In Linekin Bay. A good many have admired her from this angle.

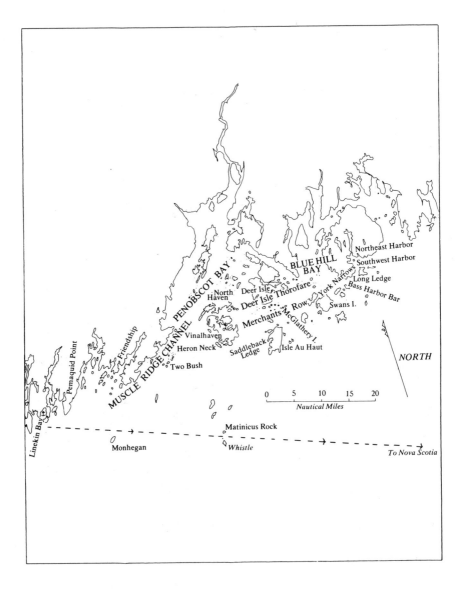

Northeast Harbor
BLUE HILL BAY
Southwest Harbor
Long Ledge
Bass Harbor Bar
PENOBSCOT BAY
North Haven
Deer Isle
Deer Isle Thorofare
York Narrows
Swans I.
Merchants Row
McGlathery I.
NORTH
Friendship
Vinalhaven
Heron Neck
Saddleback Ledge
Isle Au Haut
Pemaquid Point
MUSCLE RIDGE CHANNEL
Two Bush
0   5   10   15   20
Nautical Miles
Linekin Bay
Matinicus Rock
Monhegan
Whistle
To Nova Scotia

4   The First Night at Sea

Beating down Boothbay Harbor in the fog was an old story to us, for we had been party-boating in these waters for years. Outside, the breeze was light, the fog up a little off the gray water, and the sea lumpy and a bit confused. It was about like an afternoon sail that got "closed in on." The natural thing to do was to go back. But we were on our way to Nova Scotia to go all night, the next day and the next night perhaps. What difference did the fog make? There would be nothing to see for 150 miles and then we had a horn on Cape Fourchu and the radio station in Yarmouth to home in on. So it was thick. Need that matter?

The first problem, however, was Monhegan Island. Our course lay to the north of it past a bell and a gong. There is a powerful foghorn and a radio direction finder station on the island, so we anticipated no trouble. Still, I had serious doubts about the accuracy of the compass, which we had "not had time" to check. *How would that sound in court?* I wondered to myself.

"Captain, did you or did you not check your compass before starting on this cruise?"

"No, I did not."

"Is it generally considered the part of a responsible skipper to do so?"

"Yes."

"Could the disaster be in any way attributed to unrecognized compass error?"

"Yes."

"Why did you not ascertain the extent of the error, if any?"

"I did not have time."

The best thing to do in the presence of such doubts is to keep quiet. Either go back, wait for a clear day, and check it; or shut up and go on. We were not going back.

The breeze gradually increased until we were doing a nice four knots, sloshing along through the chop very comfortably. Occasionally the sun shone wetly through the clouds and fog. We presently picked up the radio direction finder station on Monhegan about where it should be, which is the best you can expect from a radio direction finder, and then we heard the horn on about the right bearing. The fog shut down thick. We sailed through a shoal of paper plates, ketchup bottles, beer cans, and other detritus of Monhegan civilization and minutes later picked up the bell on Sunken Duck Rock right ahead. The gong appeared soon after, although we never saw the ledge it marked or the island itself. Well, at least on an east-southeast course the compass was pretty good and the course to Yarmouth was basically east-southeast all the way.

The next mark was a whistle off Matinicus Rock twenty miles away, a close reach with the wind from the south. We had done so well on a twelve-mile piece that I had hopes we would find the whistle, even though it would be dark when we got there.

Leaving the deck to my brother and Nancy, I went below to torch up the stove. Things were rather confused in the cabin, for the last supplies had not been carefully stowed, just hove down the hatch. Also what had been stowed, I had not stowed myself so I couldn't find what I needed at once. Somehow, even though this was the first trip of the season, even though we had had no "shakedown," everything seemed pretty much as it usually was and this helped a great deal to reassure me. We were under way. Everything was all right so far. All we needed was to keep going.

Because the stovepipe was on the weather side, it was difficult to establish a draft. A hearty dose of kerosene, a spill of paper burned in the pipe, and a bucket over the smoke head did the trick. With the hash and beans cooking, a lamp lit, the table set, and the worst of the mess cleared up, the situation looked a lot brighter, warmer, and drier.

I took the wheel while Donald, Nancy, and Mary ate supper. I like it that way. It gives me the deck to myself to feel how she is getting on. As dark fell, we were marching along nicely to the east-southeast on a close reach but with sheets eased a bit, making four and a half knots very comfortably at a gentle angle of heel. The motion was rhythmic and easy with an occasional slap or buck from the odd wave top. The peapod followed docilely in the wake, taking no water and sliding around the occasional crests. Visibility was perhaps one hundred yards, the waves coming out of the grayness to windward, washing out from the lee side with a rush of gray foam, and sliding back into grayness to leeward. It seemed restricted, intimate, quite pleasant and cozy until I thought of the possible presence of other and bigger vessels running for the same buoy with the same feeling of euphoria.

Below at supper, now with Donald at the wheel, all seemed to be well in hand. Whoever put that hash in the can was a good cook. I could take off my jacket, relax and get set for the night.

At eight o'clock Mary and I took over after she and Nancy had cleaned up. As we approached Matinicus, it began to breeze up and the grayness changed to flat black. The motion became more vigorous. The seas sloshing along the lee deck turned red in the port sidelight, the fog green in the starboard. As the wave tops began to break over, they flashed and glowed with phosphorescence. Only the nearest could be seen through the fog, but with only one at a time to see, each was impressive — a bar of bright greenish light, a rushing sound, a quick lift of the vessel. Then as she settled down the back of the wave, another, longer rush of green light to leeward, fading into the black. The wake was a road of brightness with the peapod silhouetted in the midst of it.

I turned the wheel over to Mary just before nine and went below to listen to the RDF. Monhegan bore a little south of west and Matinicus Rock about east. At five after nine I caught Matinicus at east by south, just about right for the course to the whistle. By ten o'clock Matinicus was northeast a half north and Monhegan was still bearing south of west. By ten-thirty Matinicus was abeam bearing north-northeast and we were in thirty fathoms by the little red light on that reassuring new fathometer. This put us between Matinicus Rock with the light, fog signal and radio direction finder station, and the whistle. We should hear one or the other. We slacked the mainsheet, hove her to, and listened. Over the flopping of the sail and the wash of the seas we could hear nothing whatever and see no more than if we had been sewed up in a bag. Nevertheless, we had passed the Rock according to the RDF, whose confident little peeps had been moving steadily down our port side. By ten-forty the signal was about north by east and at eleven-ten we clearly heard the horn on our port quarter. We must have passed well inside the whistle and very close to the Rock.

By this time it had breezed up some more. The motion was more violent and the lee deck was full of rushing phosphorescent water most of the time. If we were to leave the deck to the other watch, we would do well to shorten sail. We were in no race, and anyway she would lose little speed with the topsail doused. I put on a safety harness, clipped on to the lifeline and worked forward. She was shoving her bow right into the steep ones and washing down the foredeck; however, I could work by the mast, braced against the pull of the harness, and had little trouble in getting the topsail on deck. She sailed more easily at once, but still charged on through the dark.

Donald and Nancy at midnight came on deck to a situation a great deal more lively than that which they had left. The vessel was going seven knots, making a tremendous noise and splash about it. The seas were bigger, noisier, and more phosphorescent than ever. Occasional schools of fish appeared like milky ways in the black water to leeward, and individual fish darted away from the crashing lee bow.

Below, it was a lot quieter and warmer than on deck, but the motion had increased. The lee bunks had collected a good deal of material which had not been stowed because it was too dark or which had fetched adrift from the weather side. Mary climbed into the after lee bunk. After moving a wet jacket and the stove lifter, I lay on the forward one.

On my first night at sea, I had learned in no doubtful way that rest is very important and that to lie down and relax, even if sleep is impossible, is worth everything later on. I was even beginning to doze off with the rhythmic motion and noise when she stuck her nose into a big one. It flooded the foredeck and drove half a bucketful down the forehatch. There was so much that it even showed phosphorescence as it came. One doesn't relax long with that kind of water in the face. However I moved, after a while I would get 'nother washing.

After an hour or so, I looked out to see how we were coming on. Donald and Nancy in safety harnesses were one dark shape by the wheel, dimly illuminated by the red binnacle light. The breeze was a little stronger, the sea a little rougher, but everything seemed to be going well. We were laying our course to Yarmouth and tearing off the miles at an encouraging rate.

On my way back to the bunk I noticed two duffel bags afloat in a puddle on the lee side of the cabin floor. I returned to the cockpit and applied myself to the pump with enthusiasm but got no suction. This was partly, perhaps, because she was heeled, but the pump intake should have been under water even so. Also it may have been because of a leaky seal or a stuck valve in the pump. With a flashlight and a screwdriver I got the pump apart and found no trouble in the valves. A piece of bicycle inner tube helped to plug the broken seal. Working a bicycle inner tube over the handle of a leaky pump in the wet and windy dark was not exactly what I had had in mind for a vacation. However, with the seal fixed and mainsheet eased so she sat up on her bottom, I pumped her out.

With the sheet eased she ran much more easily and almost as fast, so we left it that way and I turned in again.

About three a.m. I became conscious of increasingly violent motion and stuck my head out the hatch into a storm of noise and confusion. It usually seems much worse than it is, especially at night, when you come from the comparative warmth and quiet of the cabin into the outer darkness. I waited a moment to judge the conditions more objectively. My brother did not seem alarmed at all, but after I had watched it a while, it still looked pretty violent. The vessel was rolling heavily to leeward, throwing the mainsail high and then all but plunging the boom under. The sail was fully half a-luff, yet at the speed she was going in that sea she had all the sail she needed. Over the fog, lightning flickered around the northern quadrant of the horizon. The sea was a good deal rougher than it had been. I could see no great hurry so suggested we take in mainsail and jib and jog along a bit to see how things developed.

Nancy took the wheel and Don and I got the sails in without great difficulty. The jib downhaul was blessed a generous three-times-three: going out on the bowsprit — wet and possibly dangerous work — appealed to neither of us and the downhaul made it unnecessary. The mainsail with its big mast hoops and heavy gaff came down without argument as I have seen it do on some rather important occasions. We left the sail hanging in the lifts and lashed to the quarter bitts. As Claud Worth says in *Yacht Cruising*, "Time is always with you."

Jogging along under staysail is a common expedient with us and it is of great benefit to boat and crew. With the pressure of the mainsail off and only the staysail set to steady her, she does not charge the seas but rises to them. The wind can be judged at its true velocity, not its apparent velocity, and time is available for consideration.

There was one silly thing that complicated the situation. It is my habit to wear a cap on deck primarily as a defense against the sun. However, I have become so accustomed to it that even with the anchor down, I put on my cap to go on deck. Even at night I wear it. In the dark that night, I couldn't find it. It bothered me. I wanted my cap because it felt unnatural not to have it and made comparisons with other occasions difficult to assess. Dammit, I wanted my cap. My faithful wife, awakened from her doze by the lowering of the mainsail, got the message and in the confusion of the dimly-lit cabin went looking for it. She hadn't been at sea since last September, and hunting for my soggy cap in the dampness, close air, and violent motion caused her to give up her supper — after which she allowed she felt much better.

Of course she found the hat, which I installed. About fifteen minutes later it seemed that things had moderated and that the squall, if squall it really was, had passed. We surely weren't getting on very fast and although it was still rough, it was not terrifying in any way. We contemplated reefing the mainsail and perhaps we should have done so, but it did not feel like a reefing breeze.

So we set the mainsail, left the jib on the bowsprit, and carried on under main and staysail. She went very well with the mainsail about full, and the seas no longer came heavily over the bow. I stayed on deck to watch her go and she seemed to be doing very well.

By then it was four a.m. and Mary and I took over. Gradually the night faded into day. It was still thick and the seas were much bigger than last night. What we had not seen in the dark was a growing southerly roll — not steep or dangerous but impressive.

As we charged on toward Yarmouth, I got a weak RDF bearing on Mt. Desert Rock about north and one on Monhegan that was totally misleading. Then I turned my attention to the stove in which still dwelt the spark of life. When Don had gone below, he had given it a few briquets to nourish it, for a dying stove, like a starving man, may die of a surfeit. I put on the biggest pot with some water and put in four eggs, figuring that a good soaking in hot water, even if it didn't boil, would give the eggs enough substance to be eaten. An orange and a doughnut in the meantime fortified the deck watch.

I began to look ahead to the Yarmouth side of the Bay and viewed the alternatives with a considerable lack of enthusiasm. However, I know very well that four-thirty a.m. is a very poor time at which to make an important decision. Therefore, I didn't make one, but kept on east-southeast at seven knots through the fog with the lee deck swashing under and the petrels and shearwaters circling about. They seemed entirely at home and very well satisfied with the day's beginning, skipping into the hollows and swooping around the crests on stiff wings and wondering who these madmen could be.

5 Retreat

At five-thirty Donald burst from the hatch, allowing through clenched teeth that he had had about all the heaving around below that he needed. A few deep breaths of fresh air, of which there was a generous supply stirring, improved his outlook but he firmly declined a hardboiled egg, doughnut and a cup of tea.

When faced with the necessity of making a decision, the logical man considers the alternatives available, weighs dispassionately the arguments pro and con, the possible losses and the probable gains. Then he makes the wisest choice, taking such calculated risks as seem justified by the possible gain.

In this case, the logical mind was straddling the wheelbox, still wet inside his shirt from the attempt to sleep under the hatch. He was piloting a small boat through mounting seas in thick fog at a little better than hull speed. The wheels of logic ground slowly while intuition flashed a sympathetic response to the crew's clinging wet dungarees, cold feet in wet sneakers, uncertain stomachs and a long, hard day to windward ahead. After a pause for rationalization to catch up with empathy, we tacked ship and ran north for Mt. Desert Rock, still just audible on the RDF.

Later I had occasion to think over the decision at greater length, but at the moment there was no doubt that it was a popular one. I was congratulated on it then and have been since.

At once the situation improved. The motion was much easier. The decks dried off. The crew took at first a tentative interest in breakfast and then a much more positive one. We set the jib and rushed in toward Mt. Desert, surfing down the faces of the growing seas.

By eight-thirty we were getting into shoal water, we saw a lobster trap, kept off to the west to pass Columbia Ledge, and as we passed Mt. Desert Rock, heard the horn blast through the fog.

We ran on for the horn on Great Duck Island, pausing to set the topsail and again to bail out the peapod, which misbehaved abominably in the heavy following sea. She would rush down the forward side of a steep sea, her keel holding her on a straight course, and catch up with us, stopping off our quarter as the sea passed under her, her painter slack. Then as the sloop rushed ahead on another sea, the painter jerked her around almost across the face of the next sea, and, between the pull of the sloop and the rush of the wave, she raced across our stern, executing a telemark turn as her painter dragged under her bow. As she swung, she threw a great bow wave, of which she took a generous drink, and then settled into the wake again. When she repeated the process, the water she had shipped sloshed forward and magnified the next rush and swoop. Twice we hove to and bailed her.

We looked hard for Great Duck in the fog and listened attentively. The growing sea was steep enough so the light accentuated the dark backs of the waves, startling us into seeing breakers at the foot of a dark ledge and spruce trees looming over it. But the vision subsided into a wave.

On we sailed, well beyond our time, the sounder giving us a steady twenty fathoms. Surely we should hear the horn, but we heard only the slap and rush of the seas. There is nothing to hit near Great Duck, so we kept on and on, at last bursting into the circle of the fog signal's sound.

We ran in to Southwest Harbor early in the afternoon, arriving as the wind died and the rain came down in buckets. Donald and Nancy left us to return to Newagen. Mary and I, in the stark calm and thick fog, motored to Northeast Harbor, sloshed ashore in wet clothes to telephone our failure, and sloshed aboard again to find a familiar sloop nearby.   A short visit and a cheery glass of Trinidad rum started us on our way to a fire in our stove, dry clothes, a hot supper, lamplight, and bunks we did not notice were damp.

So ended our frenetic attempt to cross the Bay of Fundy.   Once rested, we thought over the experience and drew some conclusions, but for the moment we had shot our bolt.

Of the night, her first at sea, Nancy wrote:

> . . . I admit that I won't remember it as one of the most pleasant experiences of my life but it gave me an idea of what it might have been like to have been with Columbus or any other early explorer.   To be all alone enveloped in a darkness so great that it was incomprehensible was a scary feeling for me that night.   The boat was nothing as compared with the sea, wind, and darkness.   It was like a speck of dust in an old uninhabited house or one pine needle in a large forest.
>
> I am now more appreciative of sun, land, and radio signals.

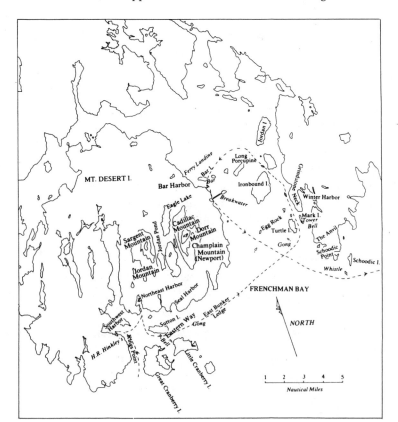

6 Reflections

We awoke in the morning to what looked like the first day of summer. Bright sun, blue sky, a light, warm, northwest breeze, and the whole State of Maine steaming from two weeks of uninterrupted fog.

We didn't move very fast. It was good to feel the sun, to eat breakfast in the cockpit, to see the decks dry, to look down the harbor to the islands outside. People were getting small boats under way, drying sails. Two little girls churned about in outboards. Over the hills surrounding the harbor, the rocky shoulder of Jordan Mountain stood gray against the sky.

Mary took everything out of the cabin — bunk cushions, pillows, sleeping bags, duffel bags, clothes, jackets, charts, everything we had stowed wet — and spread it all out to dry. We looked like a church rummage sale. I went ashore for a bath, a shave, and a haircut, for there had been "no time" for these in the rush with which we left.

Northeast Harbor was a different town from the one we had seen last night. What had been great, shallow, rain-pocked lakes through which we sloshed in sneakers had shrunk to little puddles with damp edges. The houses and streets and trees, which had loomed dripping and dull through the fog, shone bright, new-washed, sharp-edged. The whole town seemed smaller, sharper, and infinitely more friendly. Even the "Out-of-order" signs were gone from the telephones.

I found what I had come ashore for and returned bearing a big, rugged aluminum radar reflector, for which we were to be many times grateful in later weeks.

We stowed the boat all over again, and it smelled infinitely sweeter. We set mainsail and topsail, dropped our borrowed mooring, set staysail and jib, and ghosted down Northeast Harbor in the last of the northerly.

I never sail down Northeast Harbor without remembering how, many years ago on a cruise with three boys in a smaller sloop, we found our compass badly in error. On a nearby yawl was Captain Ralph Holmes, head of the physics department at the University of Vermont, a native of Ellsworth, and Maine to the toes. At a very early hour on Sunday morning he turned us out and corrected our compass for us, running courses around Greening's Island. We returned, five disreputable-looking characters on an overloaded little sloop, motoring up Northeast Harbor under the porches of the good and great, by the portholes of the wealthy dozing in their yachty staterooms, singing with a violence that shattered the Sabbath calm,

Nero my dog has fleas,
Nero my dog has fleas
From his elbows down to his knees.

On this day, however, we were happy to float out with the tide in the sunshine and to reminisce.

We had lunch outside, becalmed, waiting for the westerly: sardine sandwiches and a mug of our neighbor Hans's home-brewed cider. And we thought over the madness of the last two weeks.

Why had we left in such a hugger-mugger? Why had we not waited until the weather improved and we were properly organized? The reason was only partly concerned with an appointment we were expected to keep in Nova Scotia.

For a long time I had wanted to explore the Nova Scotia side of the Bay of Fundy. Summer after summer other considerations had interfered. In 1969 and 1970 we had tried and been stopped by fog and light, easterly airs. In 1971 and 1972 we had worked on *A Cruising Guide to the New England Coast*. At last, we were determined to go and if necessary to go in the fog. For years people have navigated the Bay of Fundy in no better vessels than ours and with equipment far less reliable. Therefore, we were determined to cross to Yarmouth, visit Meteghan where so many able fishing vessels are built, look into St. Mary's Bay, go out through Grand or Petit Passage and up to Digby to see the Annapolis Valley and the site of Champlain's second winter in America, and then cross to Saint John to thank personally several people who had been most helpful in revising the *Guide.*

We had planned to start on July first but the weather had slowed us so that we had not been ready to step the mast until June thirtieth and we had had to do it in the fog and rain. The engine had not come to life until July second and the fathometer adventure had taken place on July third. Frustrated before by postponements, I had been *determined* that it would not happen again.

In my youth, my father's brother used to borrow our sloop for a cruise each summer. He was an eager, active little man who always arrived loaded down to the axles with finer things to eat and drink than we ever saw and with several merry companions. The load was transferred aboard and the party was underway at once. One departure day I remember was dungeon-thick of fog with a suggestion of rain and wind to come. My father, a cautious person under most circumstances, suggested they lay over that night and start the next day. My uncle replied, "If you're going to go cruising, Baron, you got to go cruising," and he pushed off into the thick of it.

The late Captain E. A. McFarland, whom as boys we had loved and respected, who had lobstered in Muscongus Bay under sail, been to the Banks on big fishermen, and sailed summer and winter in coasting schooners, told us of one skipper "who would wait so long for a good chance, he'd ground on his beef bones." And he told of another who turned his crew out one morning despite a headwind, saying, "This vessel has two sides and she can sail on both of them. Get the anchor."

We had strong precedent, precept, and example in favor of rapid departure.

The worst of it, though, had not been so much the hasty start. The most regrettable part of the last two weeks had been our neglect of the things that make living in Maine worthwhile. We had been fighting the weather, the clock and the calendar. We had failed to enjoy what was there to be enjoyed, even in the fog. Now, becalmed, warm, dry and unhurried, we remembered some of the good things we had missed.

There was the day when the rains came down at noon as if the windows of heaven had been shattered. We had come to the point where we could do no more either aboard the boat or in the shop, so we ate a hot lunch and headed in the car for Sargentville where our sailmaker was finishing our new topsail.

Clarence Hale, seaman in sail, fisherman, sailmaker of remarkable skill, has made three suits of sails for *Eastward*. We found him and his son Donald, who now runs the loft, just finishing the grommets of the clew and tack. Clarence sat on a new sailmaker's bench. You seldom see a sailmaker's bench any more except in an antique store and then you find it battered and stained under dull varnish. In a mechanized world, to get a new sailmaker's bench is an act of faith. Clarence stitched in the roping on the clew by hand, driving the needle through the dacron rope and the heavy dacron tabling with a smooth motion of his whole arm, not squeezing it through with his fingers like most amateurs. I tried to follow the way he worked the hemp strands to form a loop for the brass grommet. He twisted them somehow in a way that didn't seem very clear to me and called on his grandson for a wooden fid. The third-generation Hale brought it and Clarence hammered the strands over the point to open up a hole, slipped the brass grommet in and with a small spike wound up the two ears of hemp he had left. The strands came tight around the brass. He pulled out the spike and, as if by an act of prestidigitation, the ears disappeared. He continued with the roping, tapering it by thinning out the strands little by little and re-laying the rope. Meanwhile Donald had finished the tack, made a bag, and written out the bill. We left them to start the sails for a 95-foot schooner building at Harvey Gamage's in South Bristol and headed for home on narrow roads through fields of buttercups and clover drenched in rain and dimmed by fog.

Then there was the day the engine ran. It is the tradition among stick-and-string sailormen to damn all these foul-smelling contraptions that spoil a sweet sloop, yet most of them have engines, use them extensively, and curse them fiercely when they don't run. I never really have enjoyed motoring, but there have been plenty of times in fog or calm when I have been glad indeed to hear the creature respond to the switch, and I have used it gratefully and cared for it solicitously.

At the end of the season I make it a practice to pump the cooling system full of antifreeze and then to remove all the parts which are easily unbolted and can profit from a winter in a warm, dry house rather than in the damp bilge of a laid-up boat. One advantage of this practice is that in putting things back, I have a chance to check and reseal every gasket and tubing fitting and to clean every electrical contact. Ordinarily, if I have been careful, the creature responds energetically after a few turns of the starter.

This year, however, was different. It rained and dripped fog. Between showers I carefully put the machine together — battery, starter, distributor, coil, generator, carburetor, fuel pump were all cleaned and put in place. I filed and reset the points, checked the spark plugs, timed her up. A New Harbor mechanic showed me how to do it. He held a spark plug in his hand and rolled the fly-wheel till she "squirted fire." It must have given him quite a jolt with one hand on the plug and the other grounded on the fly-wheel. Then he found out which cylinder was compressing by putting his thumb over the holes successively, and made the final adjustment by turning the distributor. I used a more conservative method of "squirting fire," but was ready at last.

I tried the starter and got no result. I choked her and fiddled with her. She barked once or twice but she wouldn't run. She even chugged several times on one cylinder, and died.

Now there is nothing deader than a dead engine. It is a corpse-cold chunk of iron smelling of gasoline, inhabited by a malevolent Caliban which sullenly resists all appeals to its better nature.

Really, I know better than that. It is a mechanical system, conceived by the mind of man and executed by his hand. It is and must be amenable to the rules of mechanics, chemistry, and thermodynamics. If it has gasoline in the cylinder, if it compresses that gasoline, if a spark flashes at the right time, then the gasoline will explode and the engine must run. Very well then. There is gasoline in the tank, in the fuel pump, in the strainer, in the carburetor. Remove a plug. There is a smell of gasoline in the cylinder and a faintly visible vapor comes out. When grounded, the plug gives a wee spark across its points, at least occasionally.

Put it all back together. Try it.

Why won't the son-of-a-bitch run?

It has the soul of a damned rat without a tail and is a creation of the Father of all Sin. Appeals to its undistinguished, vulgar, even criminal, ancestors produce no better results than careful study.

Then what haven't we thought of?

Maybe the little tubes and passages in the carburetor are plugged and the mixture is wrong. Take off the carburetor. Bring it home and dissect it, poking little wires through its holes.

Maybe it isn't compressing. Take out all spark plugs. Put your thumb over the hole of each in turn and roll her over. You can't even hold your thumb on the hole, so there is plenty of compression. Get a new gasket for the carburetor. Put it all together again. Try again — no luck. A bark or two.

Now may the devil in hell take it back where it came from. I don't want to see the illegitimate thing again. I abandon it for the night and leave beside it greasy finger marks on the white paint of the hatch coaming and rail.

The next morning I find other jobs that need doing, for I cannot face the beast. After lunch, more mature attitudes prevail. Surely there is *some* good reason why she won't go. I will approach her with confidence, think positively, act as though she had been running yesterday. She just has to go.

When I got to the yard, I found a friend who had come ashore from his powerboat. He was sitting in the front seat of his Cadillac whirling the starter with determination but getting no more results than I had with my marine engine. His battery weakened, the starter faltered, and the only sign of life was a foul smell of gasoline in the fog.

I couldn't solve my problems, but I thought I might solve his. We rigged jumper wires from the battery of my car to his, squirted silicone spray all over everything to dry off some of the accursed fog, held the automatic choker open, and by God she ran! After a few minutes of warm-up and several false starts, she was as good as new. I was dumbfounded. He was delighted. I couldn't wait to squirt that magic spray on my engine.

By this time it was late in the foggy afternoon, getting to the edge of dusk. I put the squirt to her in good shape and tried her. No result.

But what was this? From every high-tension wire came little blue sparkles. The whole top of the engine appeared bathed in flickering blue light. The wires, spray or no spray, were leaking electricity like showerheads. I went home, figuring: "Now, by God, I got you."

In the morning I rigged new wires and tried her again.

She responded like a warhorse to the trumpet. Away she went with an enthusiasm unsuspected. She warmed up, began charging her battery, circulating her oil, spitting water our her exhaust. She sang like a robin on a June morning. I cast off the mooring and took a turn around the harbor in the fog. She never missed a beat. What an ingenious piece of work is a marine engine! How beautifully contrived, how skillfully constructed, how warm and cooperative in spirit!

7 Up Frenchman Bay to Bar Harbor

Presently the southwesterly breeze came in: first a blue mistiness over the distant islands, then a hard, blue line across the silky sea, then a cool puff, a lift of the flag and a squeak of gaff jaws as we gathered way.

Under the loom of the Mt. Desert hills we ran out to East Bunker Ledge and took bearings to check our compass. To our relief, it seemed perfectly adjusted. A fishing party boat out of Bar Harbor passed, its rails lined with hopeful faces, always one in the very bow, and a shutterbug or two on the upper deck. Across Frenchman Bay loomed Schoodic Point, the Anvil, and the high shore of Grindstone Neck. There were no sails in sight over there, for Mt. Desert marks the end of many cruises. Schoodic peninsula is high, heavily wooded, and even from five miles away shows cliffs and heavy breakers. It lowers over the course eastward, forcing the eastward-bound mariner far to the south into empty ocean.

But with a fair wind and only a short run ahead to Bar Harbor where we intended to end the day, we stood across toward Turtle Island and Winter Harbor to make a good sail last. Outside the shelter of Cranberry Island we found a big old roll coming in from the south. It was a long, easy sea, hundreds of yards from crest to crest, but in the troughs, the horizon was near. We did not roll to it.

Eastward continued steadily on her way, as long and strong, swift but unhurried, the gently rounded hills flowed under us.

As we approached the eastern shore, we felt the seas steepening. Off the end of Turtle Island a sea peaked up, turned dark on the top, then lighter and lighter as the light shone through, and then slid over the ledge and subsided. Seas crested and broke in violence on the end of the island, shooting spray sometimes as high as a house, the sort of display photographers wait for with tripods and filters and later publish in engagement calendars. The tower of spray falls, spattering heavily on the ledge: at the same time the greeny-white wash has partly receded and been engulfed by the next wave, sometimes from a slightly different angle, the backwash checking the force of the incoming sea so perhaps not for five minutes will there be another such spectacular display.

A sudden roar from the quarter, a start of alarm. A half acre of white water spread behind us. The outlying ledge has tripped an unusually heavy sea. The next two or three cockle up and slide over but then a bigger one gathers up, rushes terrifically forward, cocks higher, greener, lighter, whiter, and roars over in unbelievable violence. Caught by one of these, no vessel would have a chance, for the white water is so largely air that boat and swimmer fall through it, rolled and slammed on the rock below. The speed and force with which disaster could strike is almost inconceivable.

We ran up the bay through narrow passages among the islands, the seas diminishing as we went, but always the heave and swash running under the surface, what Maine fishermen call undertow, meaning something very different from the force that pulls bathers off the Jersey beaches.

Up the bay the wind increased as the water smoothed out and it came more and more westerly off the Mt. Desert hills. We passed the cliffs of Ironbound Island, aptly named, and tacked into the upper bay where the water is smooth and blue, the wind fresh and warm off the land, and the scene is dominated by the hills. They stand in rows, rounded on top, steep and cliffy on the sides, wooded but with bare, gray granite showing through. From offshore, Champlain chose the name Isle des Monts Deserts, the island of the barren mountains. Local people called their island Mount Desert for years. Summer people, who should have known better, changed the pronunciation, but not the spelling, to Dessert, like something that follows dinner. The problem, however, never reaches a national emergency for the whole area is known outside of Maine as Bar Harbor.

Into Bar Harbor we sailed, rail awash in the puffs, passing close to a small naval vessel visiting for the July Fourth weekend. A shore party put off from her in a gross, fat rubber boat propelled by an outboard motor. It was obviously designed by an expert, for it was fast, left little wake, had enormous capacity, would not break if slammed against the vessel's side by a sea, and could be easily hoisted aboard, deflated and stowed. But it had no class at all, no style. No coxswain could be proud of that basic ugliness.

A few small yachts rolled at moorings off the town as we tacked about looking for the quietest part of the harbor, no part of which was quiet. At last we took in topsail and jib and picked up a guest mooring a hundred yards off the wharf. It was a tide-ridden, rolly, and generally unpleasant anchorage, infested by small powerboats which added their wakes to the tidal chop.

The view from the cockpit was interesting, though, in spite of annoyances. There lay a huge cement-topped wharf crowded with automobiles and people leaning on pilings. A massive float lay alongside in the swell. Party boats for fishing and sightseeing loaded and unloaded. A long, low building stood on the far side housing an information center and the harbormaster's office. Behind that, gift shops pressed in amid ice cream shops, vending machines, restaurants with rangy-dangy phonographs. Along the shore to the left on a green knoll stood a large, gracious-looking building, now a motel. The shore rose behind it in wooded slopes revealing old-fashioned houses which had escaped the great fire. Above and behind stood the hills against the sunset. To the eastward down the harbor the wooded humps of the Porcupines stood up, and between them moved the lights of the steamer *Bluenose* coming in from Yarmouth.

After dinner we went ashore for dessert. As we came up the gang-

The mate taking in the topsail. The luff of the sail is still shackled to the jackstay. (T. Gray)

way, we were met by a uniformed official who urged us to report at once to the harbormaster. He wasn't in his office but we found him in the information room chatting with one of the ladies behind the counter. He led us to his office, filled out a blank with vital information about us, told us the moorings were free and that if any messages came for us, he would see we got them. We began to feel better about Bar Harbor at once. The ladies outside were relaxed and friendly, too, in spite of the throng of tourists besetting them.

We telephoned home and discovered that our friends in Yarmouth would join us two days later via the steamer *Bluenose*, so over a gooey confection in a restaurant we planned two days of catch-up work on the boat.

We were surrounded by visitors. Variety was the only word. Here were bearded youths in tattered dungarees, shirtless or in dirty tee-shirts, looking utterly destitute, yet wearing forty-dollar walking boots and carrying new packs and blanket rolls. Families vacationing in campers strolled by, daddy leading in a light blue shirt which just failed in its mission in front. One passed in a brilliant Hawaiian print that lit up the sky. Cars from Massachusetts, Vermont, the Carolinas, Minnesota, Texas, Montana, Hawaii and Alaska! Kids splashing in the fountain, playing frisbee on the lawn. Older people walking, strolling aimlessly, fatly, languidly, thronging and choking the sidewalks, gawking into antique shops, buying coffee from machines and overcolored postcards from the racks. This is Bar Harbor, whose name calls up pictures of great white steam yachts and lofty schooners lying at anchor off mansions inhabited by the wealthy of Wall Street and Philadelphia, gay beneath the crystal chandeliers.

Bar Harbor is a busy and well-organized summer city inhabited by pleasant and patient Maine people afloat on a constantly-shifting sea of faintly frustrated, slightly disappointed travellers.

Back aboard, we lashed the peapod alongside against fenders so she would not bump in the tide, set a riding light and turned in, only to turn out again. A scraping and bumping, apparently from forward, was stilled by hauling the mooring buoy right up to the bowsprit. Then the steering gear got to rumbling and complaining in its box and was quieted. Then a loose pot cover clanked in the galley. Finally all was quiet, the stars shone down through the mosquito netting, eclipsed in patterns as the boom over the hatchway rolled through them. Water sloshed in the tank, a horn sounded from the shore. A persistent little clink made itself heard. Not on every roll did it sound, but irregularly, without pattern or rhythm, and always on the starboard roll. It was not a lamp chimney. It was near the stove. I tracked it down at last to a loose bit of firebrick inside the Shipmate, chocked it off and turned in.

8 A Day at Anchor

After a rough and disturbed night we awoke to a hot day, a brisk westerly rushing off the mountains in heavy puffs, and a host of chores.

Ashore for necessaries, we threaded our way through the lazy strollers to find a hardware store for paint thinner, masking tape, and a new brush. But it took a long walk to a store at the edge of town to find a galvanized eyebolt and thimble. The recollection of the peapod repeatedly charging our stern off Mt. Desert Rock was enough to check any weakening of resolve.

Back aboard, I got Mary started on white paint. Before we left home we had done a good deal of scraping and sanding. Now with a full quart of flat white and a new brush, she went at the scabby inside of the rail, the sides of the house, hatch covers, boom crutch, coamings, bulkhead, wheelbox — anything that would hold still long enough to be hit with a paint brush.

I took the peapod ashore with a gallon of copper paint and a roll of masking tape. I returned with what looked like a new boat, one with an eyebolt in the stern. With some white paint still in the pot, Mary painted seats and gunnel. Powerboats tearing by with people from the wharf circled us, making cutting a line with a paint brush very difficult. Let it be said to their credit that when made aware of the situation, they were very considerate, and the big party boats slipped by us always with a minimum of wash.

It was a long, hot windy day but at the end of it we looked more like a yacht than we had at the start. There was still a great deal to do, but much had been accomplished.

There are several things to be said for the owner's doing this kind of work himself, aside from the financial saving. For one thing, he gets personally acquainted with the bumps, humps, gouges and idiosyncracies of the vessel. Any soft or punky spots he discovers himself, he knows where they are, and he can decide what measures to take. For another, he can do as good a job or as fast a job as he likes. If finish is important to him, he can sand brightwork, varnish under only the most ideal conditions, and after four coats individually rubbed down he can take great pride in the job as he wipes off the salt every evening and the dew every morning. He who would rather sail can paint everything the same color so there are no lines to cut and go sailing the next day. We compromise. On *Eastward*, speaking generally, everything vertical is painted white and everything horizontal is buff. This is neat looking, involves a minimum of line cutting, and can be done with dispatch.

Rigging and engine work I rather enjoy anyway. Besides, when the wind begins to pipe up, when lanyards squeak and halyards stretch, I can look aloft with some confidence, for I personally have set up every shackle, seen to the mousing of every hook and pin, and turned in every splice in rope and wire. If anything does let go, at least I will know how to fix it.

When we first rigged the vessel in 1956 we used half-inch galvanized plow steel wire, figuring it would last as long as we did. We parceled and served the splices — that is, wrapped them with tape and marline — to keep the water out and painted them white so if the splice rusted badly, the rust would bleed through and show on the white paint outside. After several years, the galvanizing disappeared and annually we painted the wire with Rustoleum. Although a few specks of rust appeared on the servings, after fifteen years the rigging looked as good as new.

Then on a puffy northwest day we had our son John, his new wife and her parents out for a pleasant sail. They were new to the sport and a bit apprehensive when *Eastward* heeled to a puff, so with son Bill at the wheel I sat on the afterdeck holding the mainsheet with a turn on the cleat to ease her in the puffs. To windward and astern we noticed a slick, modern sloop about our size, apparently interested in overtaking the dobby old Friendship. As long as he sailed a course parallel with ours, he gained nothing; but when he bore off to converge with us, he had the wind more behind him and gained. Thus he came closer and closer on the weather side of our stern; but whenever he hauled up to pass us, he dropped back. He closed in on our weather quarter, his rushing bow just even with my seat on the stern. I looked over at him. There he stood at his tiller, staring straight ahead, as stolid as Captain Bligh, all alone in command of his ship.

I waved and commented on the nice day.

No answer, no response, only a twitch of the tiller bringing him down to within less than ten yards of us.

We weren't racing and I really had no idea how foolish he could be, so reluctantly I asked Bill to bear off a little. He followed us, thus moving the wind far enough aft so he interfered with our breeze. He slowly gained. When he was right beam, I hailed him again and stubborn as a wooden Indian he stood to his tiller.

Without a word between us, Bill and I knew what to do. As the "old salt" drew just clear of our bowsprit, Bill luffed sharply, and I trimmed the mainsheet to put us to windward of him. Just as *Eastward* swung her bowsprit at his head, with a *spung* and a thump, one of those half-inch plow steel shrouds parted and fell on deck.

Of course we luffed sharply, took in sail, and limped home. Had it happened thirty seconds earlier, someone would have been badly bumped and shaken out of his assumed calm, for we had the right of way on all counts and to save our mast, we would have had to hit him. Water had evidently run down into the splice and rusted inside the serving, as the splice was open upward.

We ordered new stainless steel wire at once, set up a rigging loft

The eyesplice in Eastward's *shroud.*

in the garage and after five days of waiting for the wire, spliced it in and re-rigged with a total loss of only eight days.

There is a good deal of satisfaction in being able to meet problems in these ways and often in a boat with old-fashioned rigging, the owner can do a quicker and better job than many modern yards. In the course of years we have replaced two topmasts, all the wire rigging, and all the running rigging. We have had the engine out twice, almost entirely dismembered it, and got it running again. The inside of the head, the running lights, tanks, and indeed the whole inside of the cabin we have installed, replaced, built or over-hauled through the years. So a day to spend at painting, doing minor rigging jobs, and generally cleaning up was a welcome oppor-tunity.

It was a long, dirty, tiring day; the motion was incessant and the hot, puffy wind was wearing, whooing in the rigging, swinging the peapod, blowing sandpaper and dust about, snapping the ensign on the stern. Going below would have been a great relief except that the bunks and floor were littered with tools, equipment boxes and spare gear being used in various projects.

By five o'clock we had had enough. We cleaned up, went ashore to buy a small steak and returned, as the heat of the sun died out, to a pleasant dinner. In the course of it we were visited by Mr. and Mrs. Derek Hamilton, bound west from Saint John for Cape Cod. They had started to beat down Frenchman Bay in the afternoon but found it too heavy and no fun so had returned. Most cruising people are interested in each other and eager to make acquaintances and share experiences. Many are the interesting people we have met just visiting around a harbor. E. B. White of the *New Yorker* stopped aboard one morning and not until later did it occur to me that "Mr. White" was the author of *Charlotte's Web* and *One Man's Meat*.

After supper we went ashore for dessert and to the movies to see *Man of La Mancha*. One does not often think of going to the movies as an appropriate way to spend cruising time; nor would I include it here did it not by its very contrast add something. Certainly there is no point in getting your soul all harrowed up by the emotional, marital or extra-marital problems of Hollywood imitations of an artificial society. But a merry picture sets a tone to the evening that is likely to enliven several days and encourage a cheery point of view, especially after a day at anchor. *Man of La Mancha* was jolly enough to laugh at, well enough sung and acted to admire, and serious enough to think about so that if one could stand the shock of emerging from melodious Spain into cacaphonous Bar Harbor, the experience fitted the cruise very well.

9 Dorr Mountain

Even in good weather there is a limit to how long it is pleasant or productive to work aboard. After packing a light lunch, we went ashore and struck through town to the south toward Sieur des Monts Spring with an idea of seeing something of the Bar Harbor side of the island.

At first it was a pleasant walk along a sidewalk under shady trees by cool lawns, flowers, and established-looking houses. Cars swished by more or less unobtrusively and we began to enjoy Bar Harbor.

Then, according to our map, a road to the right would take us over a hill and out toward the spring. It was a wilder, narrower road, turning to dirt, with occasional small houses, some with tricycles or swings in the yards, all pressed up against the road by spruce and alder growing in behind. The road did not seem to be strictly according to our map, and at length it terminated in the Bar Harbor dump, whence we fled down a path to the main tourist track. This was a wide expanse of asphalt bordered by weedy grass, beer cans, and broken bottles, the cast-offs of vacation travel. One doesn't notice it much at sixty miles an hour, but at a walking pace it is not attractive. The sun was high and hot, the road hard and glaring. Cars whizzed by, rushed by, roared by, stank by, more flashing plates from Mass., Mass., N.Y., Conn., Penna., Penna., Ore., Wash.

at us. We sought relief in the woods across the ditch and found the overgrown course of an old road, paralleling the new, with moss and indian pipes growing in the shade.

At length we found the spring, complete with a parking lot enclosed by stained logs, rustic signs with painstakingly carved letters directing the visitor to spring and museum, and finally the spring itself enclosed in an elaborate pillared gazebo and looking a bit green and warmish. A few visitors strolled heavily about, but we had the place much to ourselves.

Up the hill was the Abbé Museum, a small building with some beautifully-done murals of Mt. Desert in different seasons, a large collection of arrowheads, Indian artifacts, and relics of the early colonization of the island by French and English. A pleasant lady, Mrs. Edith Favour, was presiding. She welcomed us, almost the only visitors, told us a little about the museum and consulted with us over a trail map.

Dorr Mountain, rising just behind the museum, looked interesting and not too much to tackle so we started up. The first of it was up steps through the woods. Many of these long stairways of stone were built by the Civilian Conservation Corps during the Depression when President Roosevelt was looking for useful ways to employ young men who otherwise would have been idle. It was a worthy idea, but those steps are certainly hard work, harder even than scrambling up a trail. We were soon enough wet through our shirts and short of breath, for working on a small boat does little for the wind.

Presently the trail began to zigzag upward through brush and boulders, giving us views of the Tarn, of Newport Mountain across the valley, and of a corner of Frenchman Bay to the northeast. We felt vastly superior to the little bugs on the road below, scooting about and avoiding each other by the narrowest margins.

Finding a shady spot near a great rock, we stopped, breathless, for a sandwich and a warm gingerale. A lady and a small boy came down, informing us that we were a long, long way yet from the top. The little boy did not expect us to make it. A boy and girl passed us going up, travelling much faster than we and looking strong and tough. Sun-warmed blueberries, ripened in the thin soil, were almost too good to leave; but we pushed on.

As we got higher, the trees gave way to bushes, and we could measure our progress against the side of Newport Mountain. It was hot and heavy going but the southwest wind cooled us, and climbing granite ledges was so much better than pounding the edge of the tar! Finally we could see into Bar Harbor, even pick out the white top of our own mast. Then we looked over the top of Newport Mountain to the hazy outline of Schoodic across the bay and down on several yachts beating to the southward — one of them doubtless the Hamiltons. The slope moderated as we gained the rounded upper part of the mountain and finally we reached the top and could see Cadillac Mountain, called Green Mountain by old inhabitants, to the west of us. From its top above us came flashes of automobile windshields in the parking place. We could see specks of color, people gently strolling, admiring the view. Higher than we they were, but certainly no better satisfied. We shared a square of chocolate saved from lunch and put on the cairn a rock for each of our grandsons.

We started down the north shoulder through low blueberry bushes, gravelly places and weathered ledges, following the CCC's substantial cairns. Soon we were into the bushes, then into the high brush, at last into the woods. Mountaineers tell us it is harder going down a mountain than going up. True, it does drive your feet ahead in your shoes, pull muscles you less frequently use, and try your balance; and, true, the inexperienced mountaineer is tired from going up the mountain first, but on the Mt. Desert hills anyway, going down beats going up in every way.

Before long we came upon a brook. Without considering pollution in that pure land, we drank and in short order Mary had her feet in it, affording refreshment to spirit as well as ankles.

In the woods the trail levelled off, led us to a dirt road and then to a small tar road and so back to the Bar Harbor waterfront.

A quick dive over the side, a wash under the fresh water hose on the float, and clean clothes, followed by a meal ashore, brought a resurgence of energy and zeal.

A day ashore occasionally is a valuable part of a cruise. From the purely physical point of view, of course, it is excellent, for living on a boat is really not very hard work except for the occasional efforts like pulling the anchor or trimming the mainsheet in a breeze. Once in a week you may have to shin up the mast, but it is scarcely a regular daily effort.

The change in outlook is as important as the physical benefit. New scenery, new people, new ideas refresh the mind and spirit. To look down on your boat from a mountaintop changes your view of the mountaintop when you look up from the boat. Sailing is great, but it certainly need not be all there is to a cruise.

10 Bound East

Our two new crew members, the Birkses, were early awake as is always the case after the first night aboard. We had picked them off the *Bluenose* from Yarmouth the night before and had little more than made their acquaintance before bedtime.

As they sat at breakfast in the cockpit, balancing plate, mug and doughnut on their knees, Gerald told us that he had flown Sopwith Camels over the German lines in the First World War. The sound of the engines had damaged his hearing so he eventually became quite deaf, but he never gave in to it. He would not be left out, but listened carefully for what he could hear, tried hard to read lips, and often asked Mrs. Birks to repeat for him things others had said. He was a neatly-groomed, exact, spare gentleman with short white hair and moustache and with the quick hands and feet of an athlete and an outdoors man.

Mrs. Birks told us she had spent most of her life in a Montreal department store heading an education program for salesgirls and that she had retired from the store to marry Gerald only recently.

"Seldom," she said with restrained humor, "does a maiden lady become a grandmother so quickly."

Since their marriage they had travelled enthusiastically. One of their most difficult trips was a trek through the high country of Nepal with a group of Sherpa guides, made almost entirely on foot, this tough, game couple pushing through to the finish as eagerly as they started and taking the steep parts as they came. So here they were, embarking on a small boat with primitive accommodations under the leadership of what one of our acquaintances called "an old man and his wife" for a cruise through the hazardous waters of eastern Maine and New Brunswick.

When Mary took Mrs. Birks below to explain to her the mysteries of a marine toilet, she was a bit taken aback by the system of pumps and valves to be operated and a bit doubtful of the questionable privacy afforded by a mere curtain, but she put her hand to pump and sea-cock in proper order, and mastered her doubts about the curtain without comment.

Breakfast finished, they cheerfully plied mop and towel on the dishes and soon we were ready to make sail.

After the last two days at anchor we were glad to get under way again, taking things very slowly to show our new crew the ropes. Gerald wanted to understand everything, helped set sails and quickly learned the leads of halyards, sheets and downhauls.

With a warm westerly still blowing, we slipped out of Bar Harbor with great relief and headed off Egg Rock in order to round Schoodic Whistle and head down east. As the wind softened, we gazed at the elaborate cottages along shore and remembered how the *Leviathan*, then named the *Deutschland*, put into Bar Harbor in 1914 to avoid capture by the British. She was not only a valuable ship but had German gold aboard.

Mary got a fishline over the stern and as the breeze slackened further, caught a mackerel. She is a relentless fisherman and absolutely tireless. She told the Birkses how some years ago a storekeeper in Round Pond, Maine, invented a lure which was simply five white nylon flies on a nylon leader with a spoon or spinner on the end. It proved to be lethal to mackerel. It was irresistible. You couldn't sail up Muscongus Sound trailing one without catching a pailful of mackerel — unless of course there were none there. If you caught none, it proved that there were none present. The Birkses doubted the yarn; but when Mary scored in the first ten minutes, they doubted their doubts. Half an hour later, two more mackerel came over the side at once and that clinched it.

We looked up at Dorr Mountain with new understanding, for just the day before we had been there and we knew how steep were the sides. Mary had been so exhausted she had had to do some of the steep parts on hands and knees. The flesh may have been a bit on the weak side, but the spirit was indomitable. With the glasses we could see the cairn on the summit, almost pick out the rocks we had left for our grandsons. So now Dorr Mountain was part of our lives as it had not been when we sailed into Bar Harbor.

Presently a cool, salty draft of southerly came in, the topsail and then the lower sails filled, and we were on our way. Gerald took the wheel, soon got the hang of it, and steered small. Off Schoodic the wind eased again.

We have noticed that this generally happens off the windward side of an island or point, especially if it is a lofty one. Cape Rosier, Isle au Haut, Mosquito Island, Monhegan, Pemaquid Point and Squirrel Island are just a few of the notorious dead spots on the coast. A professor of meteorology, Charles F. Brooks of the Blue Hill Observatory, explained the phenomenon to me once and I included the explanation in the *Guide*. Suffice it to say here that we hit a soft spot.

We sogged along in the tide and light air toward Schoodic Whistle, visible but almost inaudible. Of course we could have started up the engine and gone on our way, but there were strong arguments in my mind against such a decision. First, we were in no desperate trouble. A great many people in America would have been delighted to sit on a boat in Frenchman Bay contemplating the Mt. Desert Hills. The sea was a little sloppy but not uncomfortable. If we started the machine, we would add its rhythmic pounding to the scene and blank out the sounds of water and boat. Our attention would perforce be concentrated on clock and compass. The motion would be more insistent. Conversation would become difficult and the quality of the day would be changed. True, we would be "getting somewhere," but even if we lay becalmed all day and finally fanned into Winter Harbor, we could get somewhere. Winter Harbor is an interesting spot if you approach it with an interested mind.

Also it was the Birkses' first day. They had driven from Montreal to Saint John, left their car and crossed to Digby, made their way up the shore to Yarmouth, waited for us there, and finally crossed to Bar Harbor, pushing eagerly all the way to join us. I did not want them to keep pushing to get somewhere else. We were bound for Saint John, but the purpose of the cruise was really not to arrive at Saint John but to have a good time getting there. They must be given a chance to slow down, unwind, and learn to enjoy what was around them.

So although the peapod painter fell slack, the fishline tended downward on a steep angle, the bubbles passed slowly and the mainsheet occasionally rolled slack, dragged in the water and snapped cool drops on us, we started no engine. Gradually the breeze picked up from the south-southwest. The peapod settled into the wake, the fishline slackened and then was taken in. The sea became more regular, the motion less. The haze thickened and we settled down on the course for Petit Manan about eight miles away. Had we run the engine, we would have been slow to shut it off, for it is a hypnotic creature, and we could have missed the pleasant transition from calm to a fair wind.

Shortly after noon the haze thickened up and the breeze increased so that we were washing along between five and six knots, out of sight of land. There isn't anything much to see in that stretch of coast between Schoodic and Petit Manan anyway. Bunker Harbor, Prospect Harbor and Corea are far to leeward. The Black Rocks, the Old Man and the Old Woman are steep, rugged ledges rising out of heavy breakers and, while very impressive from a quarter of a mile, are not much to look at from far offshore. Dyer Bay and Gouldsboro Bay run far up into the land but their entrances are all but invisible. The shore appears distant, lonely and almost uninhabited.

About twelve-thirty we began to hear the fog horn on Petit Manan blasting on our port bow about where we expected it. Petit Manan is a long, low island extending from a long, low point. It is fringed with ledges which extend far outside the island and break heavily in rough weather. The tide runs east and west along the coast with the flood and ebb but also runs in and out of Narraguagus, Pigeon Hill, and Pleasant Bays on the west. Therefore the sea is always sloppy and confused for several miles outside. The scene is dominated by the lighthouse, a lean, brown granite tower rising over 120 feet above the low island.

We saw it through the haze as we ran by the bell buoy a mile off the island and then it quickly disappeared astern, the horn to windward now, sounding louder than before, almost explosively at the beginning of each blast.

Again we were out of sight of land. Except for two buoys on Tibbets Rock, a four-fathom ledge miles from land, there was nothing ahead for a dozen miles. We moved eastward in a vague circle of visibility about a mile in radius, the sun shining warmly down on us, the wind fair, the sea quite smooth and regular, although with an increasing heave. The sails were full and quiet except for the occasional slam of the staysail traveller. The compass hung steadily on east three-quarters north and we rolled along.

Gerald took a spell at the wheel and then a bit of a nap below out of the sun. Mrs. B chocked herself in a corner of the cockpit and, at ease, told us something of her experiences teaching in Montreal. The brave southerly breeze kept on with its good work and we tore off the miles eastward.

Occasionally we passed a big offshore lobster buoy and noticed the flood tide making briskly in our favor, sometimes nearly pulling the buoy under. Lobstermen in able offshore boats occasionally swung into our circle, hauled a trap, waved cheerfully, and dropped astern.

About three o'clock a lonesome bell showed up to port, slamming in the swell, marking Sea Horse Rock breaking near it. Shortly after, a whiteness loomed through the haze that took on the outlines of

Crumple Island, a bare, white granite dome like a huge cauliflower nearly 100 feet high, the sea hammering the dark line at its foot, the gulls hanging over it on the wind, and colonies of cormorants peppering its surface. It is as lonesome as Petit Manan but in a different way, for it entirely dominates the scene. Here the land comes to a full and dramatic stop. Outside lie cold water, fog, storm, and Fundy tides. Inside lie bare heath, spruce woods, coves, islands, and finally the houses and boat shops of Jonesport.

Pond Head, Red Head, Freeman Rock, Mistake Island, Man Island and Black Head are all the same sort of limits — definite, powerful, commanding.

After rounding these, we trimmed sheets and worked into the lee of Head Harbor Island where we found smoother water, less wind and the land beginning to reach out around us. Buoys were closer.

Looking forward.   Note the jib topsail tied up on the whisker shroud, the topsail sheet hanging on the boom jaws, and the jackstay set up with a little tackle at the foot of the mast. (Prenatt)

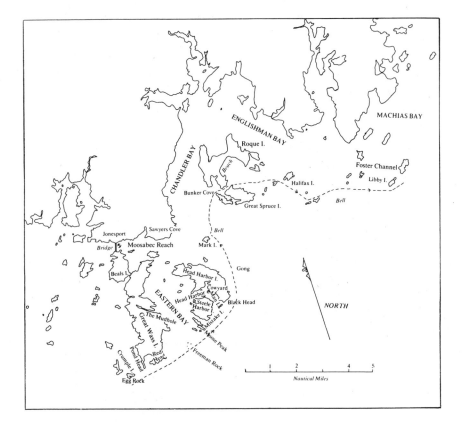

MACHIAS BAY

ENGLISHMAN BAY

Roque I.

Foster Channel

CHANDLER BAY

Beach

Halifax I.

Libby I.

Bunker Cove

Great Spruce I.

Bell

Bell

Jonesport

Sawyers Cove

Mark I.

Moosabec Reach

Bridge

Gong

Beals I.

Head Harbor I.

Cowyard

NORTH

Head Harbor

Man I.

EASTERN BAY

Steele I.

Harbor I.

Black Head

The Mudhole

Mistake I.

Great Wass I.

Moose Peak

Pond Head

Freeman Rock

Crumple I.

Red

Head

Egg Rock

1   2   4   5

Nautical Miles

The familiar wooded mound of Mark Island rose ahead. The fields and houses of Jonesport appeared comfortably to port. To starboard the dark spruce shores of Roque Island were sharp in the late light. About five o'clock we took in topsail and jib and slipped quietly into the entrance to Roque Island Thorofare. Crows rose protesting from the shingle. An osprey circled overhead. The tide, almost high, carried us quietly, becalmed behind the hill, into the mouth of Bunker Cove where we anchored with great satisfaction. The log of this day concludes, "This is something like a cruise."

The Birkses, after a day of new experiences and new strains, relaxed too.

We had not seen a yacht all day long. It had been a hard year to fit out, but even so there are usually a few hardy mariners sailing on Frenchman Bay, running east to Petit Manan and Crumple Island or holed up at Roque. Yet none were here. We felt as if we were finding it for the first time and it was perfect.

We took a short walk ashore, for we had something to show the Birkses that we had not spoken of. In the peapod we rowed to a rocky beach and followed a trail through grassy swales and thick spruce woods, fighting voracious mosquitoes, and came suddenly on a long, white beach. A crescent of finest sand a mile long lay before us, protected from the sea, clean, cold and with a perfection of line and curve, color and form, that is breathtaking.

11 Codfish

The next morning to get back into our cruising routine, Mary and I dove overboard before taking time to test the water or consider the implications of July in the Bay of Fundy. It was paralyzing but I really believe we got out faster than we got in. Never swim in the Bay of Fundy. Yet we have always made a habit of going overboard, because the resolution necessary to put on a bathing suit, sometimes a wet one, to stand on the rail and make the plunge, marks an end to the night and a beginning to the day. When I used to cruise with boys, it was a great way to get the boys out of their sacks. The dip was not "required," but the most powerful and subtle pressures were applied. I made a point of being the first one in on the first morning of the cruise and thus became the Grand Eagle of the Ancient Order of Morning Eagles. Anyone could become an eagle by wanting to swim before breakfast and expressing his desire by doing so. Anyone who skipped more than one day was judged by other eagles as being no longer desirous of going in. In very bad weather the eagles in good standing could vote it "no day" and skip a day; and all rules were off in the Bay of Fundy, which is really too cold for eagles.

The effect of all this foolishness was to get the crew out of their bunks and on deck in the morning. After a dip, they lost no time dressing and I could get breakfast and move the day along. Otherwise, I sometimes had to poke people with a cooking fork to get the day going. We became addicted to the practice and now really enjoy it, although few of our guests are interested.

It was a cool, clear morning without a breath of air and with an overcast beginning to creep up from the southwest. The ladies, who had collected some plants the day before in a coffee can, went ashore to explore and to seek the proper soil for their garden. I went to rigging our new topsail, leisurely enjoying the lack of pressure. Gerald, by far the most productive of the crew, began a pen and ink sketch of a tiny tree-capped island which protected our anchorage from the northwest. It carries in itself the isolation, the uncultivated beauty, the toughness and the peace of eastern Maine, and Gerald had just the touch to bring these out. One hates to gape over an artist's shoulder. Yet I stole quick glances as I went below for a ball of marline or poked into a locker for a bit of sail twine. Presently he finished it, put it away, and began a watercolor.

The ladies returned from their shore excursion, the topsail was ready to set, and there was still no wind; but it seemed like a good time to get under way. It was not — emphatically. There was no particular immediate destination. There was no wind. The tide was against us. We had plenty to eat, a full rum bottle, and were anchored in a most beautiful anchorage. Furthermore, and most importantly, Gerald was creating something that would have given him and everyone who saw it more pleasure than we would get by motoring to the eastward for an hour.

However, we started off under power and threaded our way through shoals and ledges out to Libby Island, an offshore island at the entrance to Grand Manan Channel. It is a cliffy island, grassy and bare except for the light station. In the shoal water off the southern end two men from Bucks Harbor in Machias Bay were anchored in an outboard jigging for codfish. We suggested buying some of their catch but they had only two and felt very strongly that they should take those two fine codfish home to their waiting wives and that no amount of money we cared to put up would balance the distress in which they would find themselves should they return to Bucks Harbor empty-handed. "My wife would kill me," said one.

We had abandoned the idea of motoring across to Grand Manan, a good four hours away to the eastward, so beat slowly against the tide in front of the lighthouse, only just holding our own.

What registered with Mary, though, had been those two codfish. If codfish were to be caught, she would be the one to catch them. She dug into the locker and came up with a codline. We use a heavy, tarred line about an eighth of an inch thick with a jig on it, a piece of lead eight inches long shaped like an elongated diamond and chrome-plated. On the lower end of the lead are three big hooks in a cluster. You let it down to the bottom, raise it a foot, and yank it up and down. Presumably the codfish, curious about this flickering herring-like thing, comes to investigate and is hooked under the chin, even if he does not try to make a meal of the lure.

I didn't have much hope for a codfish on an ebb tide with a light jig, but Mary, as her nature dictates, persevered. She would hear no gloomy prognostication of defeat but first asked that we slow the boat almost to a stop. Then she swung the jig and hurled it as far ahead as she could. As *Eastward* moved slowly up to the line, she slacked off and had a chance for a few jigs before the line was towed clear of the bottom. If it would amuse her and the Birkses, thought I, what could be the harm in trying?

About the third try she began to pull in fast, announcing the imminent arrival of a fish on deck. Then it got off. Alas. But it probably had been only a kelp or a chunk of weed, anyway.

Twice more she connected, but no fish came to the surface and you can't put a bite in the pan. I suggested she jig harder and keep pulling hard once the fish was hooked. In desperation and with lacerated pride, she let me try. About the third yank the line fetched up hard against something. I pulled in fast to keep the tension on. Finally down through the green water there showed a white flicker. Then to the surface came a fine reddish-brown codfish that I hoisted aboard and dropped icy cold on the cockpit floor to my own and everyone's surprise. So I tried again and got another. That was all we could eat, but Mary was not to be "skunked" so she tried for one and got the biggest of the lot. Three fat codfish, weighing perhaps six or eight pounds apiece, would make us a better supper than we could buy anywhere.

As the tide turned, the haze began to close in and the clouds thickened. A good little easterly air came in and took us up toward Cross Island but it died away again and at last we had recourse to the engine for we were seven miles from the very attractive town of Cutler where we expected to find good friends, a store, and a telephone. Before we made it, however, the breeze came in again and we sailed gently up that lovely harbor. It is shaped like a bottle with Little River Island the loose-fitting cork. The shores are high and wooded except on the southwest side where a classic downeast farmhouse stands on a grassy knoll with the woods coming down behind it. On the northerly side lies the town, its single street running along the shore with wharves on one side and small, snug houses on the other. Some are old-fashioned Maine houses with steeply-pitched roofs and others are more modern "ranch-type" houses. Somehow the Western motif seems out of place here on the eastern edge of the country, but "ranch houses" are all over the earth now, wherever prefab has extended.

As soon as we anchored, we were visited by two friendly girls in a skiff who seemed interested in seeing the boat. We welcomed them aboard and they told us about the botanical exhibits we had found at Roque Island. Then one of them mentioned in a subdued voice the loss of a young lobsterman the previous week.

It had happened on the same day that we had crossed Frenchman Bay on the way to Bar Harbor and seen the heavy surf on Turtle Island. He had recently been married, had a job teaching school in Cutler for the fall, and was lobstering in a skiff with an outboard along the cliffs. As he was hauling his traps, the seas were building up in the wake of Hurricane Alice. Apparently he went in too close after a buoy and was caught and smashed by a big sea. His boat broke in half, the bow and a life preserver floating out. Another lobsterman recognized it and radioed the Coast Guard. They found the stern of his skiff and his body in the surf. The whole community was sobered by the loss, and it affected us too, for we realized again how swiftly an apparently insignificant action can join with an unfortunate combination of circumstances to turn adventure to disaster even in a society which has to such a large extent "conquered" nature.

As we were talking, suddenly the Fundy fog came down over island, hill and harbor, choking thick and soaking wet. Just as it did, a great white power cruiser glided by us bound out in the deepening dusk. Her boxy hull was surmounted by bridge, flying bridge and hurricane deck with a radar whirling around on top of all. On the foredeck a hand was mopping off anchor mud. I asked him where he was bound and he made circular gestures, his fingers to his ears, suggesting that he and the management were not in sympathy. As the great square stern drew by, we read *Silver Shallis* — horrid pun?

Less than ten minutes later horns began blowing in the dusk from up the harbor and down. We at once began banging our bell, the signal for a vessel at anchor in the fog, and lost no time in rigging our radar reflector. *Silver Shallis* slipped invisibly by and, warned off the other anchored yachts by everything from air horns to fry pans, at length came to a quiet and sensible anchorage which she should never have left.

12   Building Eastward

The next morning dawned wet and windy so we let it dawn by itself. By quarter of eight there was no improvement, but we turned out, cooked breakfast on the Shipmate stove which warmed us up and dried us out, made a leisurely ceremony of eating, and with the dishes washed and things pretty well stowed away, settled back to talk it over.

Gerald asked about the boat. Why had we chosen a Friendship sloop and how had we come to get *Eastward*? With the morning ahead of us, I told him the whole story.

It began in 1925 when my father had Goudy and Stevens in East Boothbay build for the family a round-bowed 28-foot sloop named *Dorothy*. We used her for years, cruising the coast from New York to Grand Manan. When I grew old enough, I sailed cruising parties of boys on her and through the experience learned a great deal.

Finally, in 1953, my father sold her with the idea of having a larger boat built. S. S. Crocker of Manchester designed a cutter for us, but she somehow never got started. Our twins were twelve by this time and their "little" brother was nine, a gang that should have been triplets. They could all swim, had learned to row a punt and sail a Turnabout, and were ready for the sort of experience my brother and sisters and I had had on the old *Dorothy*. No progress was being made on my father's new boat, so it became apparent that if we wanted a boat, we would have to get one ourselves with our own limited resources.

The only way possible to purchase and support a boat seemed to be through sailing day parties. We obviously could not afford a boat big enough to cruise with the whole family and a paying party, too. Therefore, a boat big enough for eight or ten day passengers which could be handled by a man and a small boy seemed the thing. The boys could rotate as crew and thus each gain experience. Once in a while we might go off for a cruise if we could get ahead financially.

I had sailed in Friendship sloops as a boy and admired them, so we had a Friendship in mind when we started looking in August for a suitable boat. We found very little. Most of the old boats were so old that we would not want to go off to Monhegan in one lest she open up like an old basket. One man snorted at the suggestion of a Friendship sloop, spat over the edge of the wharf and said deliberately, "Any man with a Friendship sloop owns a pair of trailboards, a pile of rot, and a damned good pump."

Then came two hurricanes in succession, putting some more Friendships out of consideration. We gave up temporarily and went back to the winter's business at school.

On the day before the Columbus Day weekend I had a telephone call from a broker in Boothbay Harbor.

"Oh, Mr. Duncan, I have just found the boat for you. She is thirty-two feet long, has all been rebuilt, is in first-class shape and is available right now at a very reasonable price. But you better make an offer right away because another party is looking at her." I never bought anything very big that was not being immediately threatened by another party.

So Friday night I drove to Maine in the little blue Ford pick-up we owned at the time and on a lovely fall Saturday went to inspect what I was ready to believe was our new boat.

This sort of situation is supposed to be love at first sight. Creston Bryant, the yard owner, introduced us. *Venturer* looked tired. She lay on her cradle, a frayed halyard hanging limply from her mast, and greeted me feebly. I walked around her. She did have a nice bow and a pretty, flat run. I began to see through the dowdy paint and to get interested. But the stern had been rebuilt and looked clumsy and she was closer to twenty-eight than thirty-two feet long.

I went aboard. Pools of rainwater lay in the angle between the house and the deck. My knife found punky wood there. Surely this could be easily fixed up. I poked around below. She had leaked badly through the deck. The stern had rot in it. My knife went out of sight in the stem.

I found Creston and got him to come aboard and talk about a new stem, and some new deck beams. We sat opposite each other on the two bunks with the cabin floorboard picked up between us, talked about the possibilities and idly poked at her with knife points. I jabbed the mast, encouraged to find it sound. Creston jabbed the keel next to the mast step and lifted out a teaspoonful of rot. A glum silence descended on the October day.

"Say, why don't you get someone to build you a bare hull and then buy an old wreck like this and put the rigging and gear into the new hull?"

The sun struggled through clouds.

"It would cost too much to build a new boat."

"No it wouldn't. Winthrop McFarland in Christmas Cove would build you one for $100 a foot."

The sun shone through.

"One hundred dollars a foot is $3,200 for a thirty-two foot boat. We could swing that. Where is this guy?"

I banged down the Christmas Cove road and began to inquire for Winthrop McFarland. Everyone knew him but no one knew where he was on that lovely Saturday afternoon. Finally:

"Him and his brother, they're shingling the church."

I found the church. High on the roof perched on a staging was someone banging away at shingle nails with an enthusiasm that suggested he could build a sloop in a month.

"I'm looking for Winthrop McFarland," I shouted from the ground.

"Well, you came close. I'm his brother."

"Where can I find him?"

"If they ain't hung him yet, you'll find him out in the middle of the river on that yacht, drinking beer." He gestured with his hammer.

Steaming up and down the Damariscotta River in front of Christmas Cove was a small power cruiser towing a dory and manned by a cockpit-full of merry fellows.

So I sat on the wharf and waited for the situation to resolve itself.

An hour later someone hauled the dory alongside and headed for the float, standing up and rowing cross-handed. If it wasn't Winthrop, at least it was a Maine man. The dory bumped alongside and Winthrop set several quart bottles of ale on the float. We sat down beside them, our feet in the dory, each with a bottle in hand, and began —

"I'm looking for a sloop to sail parties."

"What kind of a sloop?"

"Oh, around thirty-two feet. Maybe a Friendship?"

"They ain't any more of them around that's any good."

"I know where I can get an old one. Creston Bryant said maybe you could build me a hull to put the rigging and gear in."

"Sure, I can, if I don't take a job at Harvey Gamage's, building draggers."

Over the falls I went.

"When can you start? Tomorrow?"

"Now wait a minute. I got to have a set of lines first."

"Where do I get a set of lines? Don't you build from a model?"

"No. I got to have a set of lines to make patterns and molds from and all that."

"Well, where do I get lines?"

"There's a fella up in South Bristol can draw lines, fella named Peterson. Why don't you go see him?"

So off the little blue truck banged again, up the road to South Bristol.

I drove into Mr. Peterson's driveway by his gracious yellow house looking over a field to Jones Cove and the east bank of the river. I beat on the door and a big pleasant man answered.

"Winthrop McFarland is going to build me a sloop. He needs a set of lines. Could you do it?"

Murray Peterson led me up the winding stairs to his drafting room and I suddenly realized on whom I had come crashing in so unceremoniously. On the walls were dozens of half models and pictures of vessels. I recognized several, among them ones I had long admired — the *Coasters*. These were beautiful schooners built in the tradition of the New England trading schooners of the last century but developed and modified as yachts. Murray Peterson was one of America's foremost yacht designers, an artist and an engineer, a combination unbeatable. And I had just busted in and asked if he could draw me a set of lines!

Well, he certainly could. He had long been interested in developing yachts from traditional workboat designs. Besides coasters he had done others but never had he done a Friendship sloop. His enthusiasm grew as we talked.

I needed a boat with a big cockpit, one you could sit down in and not feel as if you were falling off when she heeled. She must be dry. She must sail pretty much on her bottom rather than her side. She must be fast enough to be fun to sail, handy enough to sail about in harbors and come up to floats, and she must be rigged so a man aft and a boy forward could handle her without running back and forth through the cockpit and climbing all over people. She must have an engine to get people home on schedule, and finally, she must be good-looking.

"Do you want a topsail?" Do I want a topsail? Will a rock drop down a well? "Of course I do, but we can't afford it so draw it in and we will add it later."

We talked of materials — pine or oak or Philippine mahogany. We discussed ballast, inside or outside. Keep her simple, I said. No outside ballast.

"That's quite a mainsail you'll be playing with, Mr. Duncan."

So an iron keel. For she must carry sail enough to move her in light airs even if we would have to reef earlier than some.

The afternoon faded into evening. I climbed back into the truck and left in the early dusk, practically the owner of a sloop.

Two weeks later came a manila envelope with a breathtaking drawing. It was lovely in every way, from every angle. From clipper bow the sheer swept cleanly to a tucked-up fisherman stern. The proportions of spar and sail were exactly right. At once we agreed Murray should draw up construction plans.

By mid-November he was far enough along for me to go see Winthrop again. But Winthrop had a job with Harvey Gamage and could not build the boat. Murray and I travelled and called and wrote. My ally Hugh Williams of Bremen, Maine, spent afternoons, evenings and weekends exploring yards I could not get to. Everyone was either too expensive or already committed for the winter or both. Again the project slowed down.

New Year's Eve Murray called me in Concord. He had found a builder.

The next day I drove down and we called on Jimmy Chadwick in his shop at Pemaquid Beach. It was cold in the shed. Along one side and one end stretched a long bench with several vises. A band saw and a bench saw stood knee deep in sawdust, chips and short ends. The bench was crowded with paint pots, coffee cans of nails, a ball of caulking cotton. On ways at the lower end of the shed stood a small powerboat. She looked neat and trim. The planks came cleanly to the stem and fitted the frames without gaps. The boat had been built by a man who did things right.

"Well, no, I never built a sloop that big," said Jimmy, "but I've always wanted to and my father has built lots of them. He would help me."

We got talking about fastenings: copper or galvanized.

"I should think galvanized would be good enough," I said. "The old *Dorothy* is fastened with galvanized nails and after thirty years is sound as ever."

"That was probably Swedish iron," said Murray.

Jimmy reached into a coffee can for a galvanized boat nail, spun the vise tight on it, and hit it sideways with the hammer. He tossed it to me. The galvanizing had peeled off where it had bent.

"How much more for copper?" I asked.

"About $90."

"I could make $90 in two days sailing parties. Make it copper." So it was copper nails, clinched.

The discussion continued for another hour and then I asked, "When can you start?"

"First, I must raise the roof and build a second floor on the shed to have a big enough floor to lay out the plans full size and make molds and patterns. By the time that is done, the timbers should be here and we can start in."

I left Jimmy a substantial deposit.

In mid-February I wrote. It had been awful cold, too cold to lay up bricks in the chimney or lay shingles on the roof, but a new floor had been laid in the shed.

"That's more of a boat than Grampa has," observed an astute son.

By mid-March there was a tangle of partly-shaped, heavy, rough timber in the shop, Jimmy chipping away with an adze at the stern post, one neat little "chip" after the other, each stroke under perfect control.

By April nineteenth the backbone was set up, the confusion of heavy timbers now bolted in orderly pattern, every joint straight and tight.

Then came molds and battens and we could see the shape she was to take. On May thirtieth I came into the shop to find Jimmy sawing off the sheerstrake to the curve of the sheer.

From here it was frustratingly slow. We had bought an old sloop, *Islander*, from a minister for a trifle on condition that we never put her overboard, for she was far gone and the conscientious clergyman did not wish to be responsible for my demise. We took out the engine and bolted it to beds in the new boat. We cleaned up the ballast. We got the steering gear, head, bowsprit, gaff and boom.

We steamed mast hoops and bent them around a log. We used what wire we could from the old boat, bought a lot of new wire and spliced in the upper ends of all the rigging. All this we did and much more. It was a busy summer but there was no launching.

Framing the deck was a bigger job than I had imagined. Every piece had to fit into several others and not just butt up against them either. For instance, the short pieces supporting the side deck between coaming and rail were notched into the deck clamp at the side, bolted to the top of a frame and then dovetailed into the fore-and-aft piece that formed the side of the cockpit. The whole affair was decked over and is now completely invisible, yet Jimmy knows how she is put together and so do I.

At the partners, too, where the mast goes through the deck there are pairs of heavy oak knees between the deck beams, bracing the beams against clamp, shelf and frames so the combination of mast, rigging, and deck is all one rigid truss heavily bolted together and fitting so closely no knife blade can slip between the heavy timbers.

On Labor Day we had a boat but she was still not ready to launch.

All winter we collected ballast — streetcar rails, the castings from an old piano, engine heads, pieces of an old boiler we broke up with a maul.

On the high tides in May, Jimmy hauled her down on the flats and she floated in her cradle.

In June, 1956, we stepped the mast, seized up the lower ends of the rigging, stowed ballast and sailed away.

We had about half a boat. By August we were sailing parties sitting on orange crates and planks and we have been finishing her ever since. We added the topmast, extended the house, put in a new engine, finished out the cabin, and are still "improving" her. She has been better than we had dreamed she could be — fast, handy, supremely good-looking.

All the while I was telling the yarn, Gerald had been working with his pencil. He showed me a portrait of the skipper sitting next to the stove. At any rate, the morning had produced something to show.

13   Digressions Afloat and Ashore

I stood up and looked out the companionway at the water sloshing
on the cockpit floor and the radar reflector dripping on the end of
the boom. The easterly still blew in cold and wet off the Bay of
Fundy. Little River Island loomed dimly through a veil of rain at
the harbor's entrance; the high insistent note of the fog signal on the
lighthouse complained steadily of the fog outside. The other yachts
lying at anchor moved uneasily in the harbor chop and dripped.
No one was in sight, afloat or ashore. Had it not been for the Shipmate which warmed and dried us, it would have been a miserable
scene indeed.

So we had a lunch of black bean soup, bread and cheese, and
projected a trip ashore. Once we were on deck dressed in oil clothes,
somehow the day seemed much more cheerful. Wearing sneakers
thoroughly soaked from bailing out the peapod is not nearly as bad
as standing in dry sneakers thinking about getting them wet. The
Birkses, wearing their new oil clothes for the first time, felt a little
self-conscious but very glad to have them.

With a package of letters to mail and the trash bucket, we rowed
ashore to land at a slippery little float, now aground at low water,
and a long flight of stairs to the top of the wharf. I knew those
stairs from previous visits. Submerged most of the time, the lower

steps were slimy, but some ingenious person had nailed hardware cloth over the roofing paper treads and provided a firm footing.

The little post office gulped our letters. It was like all the other village post offices — one wall devoted largely to boxes, each with its black and gilt number and its combination lock. A window and counter afforded a view of the interior occupied by two canvas mail-bags, a formidable safe, a geranium and a cheerful postmistress interested in our voyage, the weather, and our needs. Now that the government in its wisdom has insisted that post offices be separate establishments from stores, you buy stamps here and cards next door.

The store was not a great deal bigger than the post office. The storekeeper found little for us in his refrigerator except hamburg frozen harder than Pharaoh's heart and some good cheese. Meanwhile the crew looted the shelves, coming up with a canned ham and a fruit cake in a Christmas-y tin box. Bread we would have bought but there was none except the very soft store bread that simply can't stand up to a dollop of peanut butter. It goes all to pieces under the knife. I know we could bake better bread in the Shipmate if we ever took the time to experiment a little. People have.

Also cards. We bought a stack of brilliantly colored views of Cutler which nourished our faith that the sun does shine there sometimes and that the northwest wind blows dry and clear. These were hastily written and fed to the post box. Two local people dropped in to the store, talking about Watergate. In the books, fishermen always wear rubber boots and oil clothes and talk in a thick dialect about the weather and the prospects for lobsters. As a matter of record, however, citizens of Cutler listen to the same news and the same weather reports that the rest of us hear, read the same magazines, and are as upset as Bostonians about reprehensible behavior in Washington. These gentlemen offered nothing new on the subject, however, and I was so sick of Watergate that I merely asked the whereabouts of the Corbett brothers, who had written me about Cutler for the *Guide*.

We turned off the narrow tar road above the harbor, splashing down a puddly driveway to a wharf. There seemed to be no one about, and the dampness struck in through the oil clothes. However, a light burned in the fish house and there I found Neil Corbett dressed in a black and green checked lumber shirt and studying an engine manual. It seems a local summer resident had bought a little Friendship sloop with a tiny toy of an engine, tucked inaccessibly beneath the cockpit floor. It had run for a while on the delivery trip but now had signed out completely. Neil had followed up the pipes and wires and found them all different from the diagrams in the manual so we tried to unravel the tangled skein. As an English teacher, I thought perhaps I could contribute some understanding of the language to Neil's knowledge of engines, but we did not accomplish any signal victory, for like many instruction books, this one was written by someone who understood the machine so well that he was incapable of believing that anyone could be puzzled by it. The manual was the essence of clarity to the man who already understood the engine, but to the man who had just bought it, the explanation was incomprehensible. We gave it up when Neil's brother Myron came in.

Myron had been on coasting schooners in his youth and had known many of their skippers and crews. He had written about them and was in the process of putting together a collection of yarns, so it would be ungenerous to repeat any here. When the book comes out, however, I want to be first in line. I would like the whole story of the boy who went to Calais to ship on a schooner and cannily chose one with a rusty pump handle, figuring she didn't leak. They hadn't got down the river to Robbinston, however, before the skipper produced another pump handle, well-worn and shiny, and set the watch to pumping. It was calm so the skipper threw some crocus bags into the yawl boat and sent the boy and another hand ashore to fill them at the manure pile of a local farm. The manure, dumped over the bow as the vessel sailed slowly along, would be sucked into the open seams and plug them temporarily. A good dose down the rudder port was said to be helpful, too. Read Myron's book when it comes out and find out what the boy said.

Both brothers had lived long in eastern Maine and had much to tell about fishing under sail and power, about the tides, the gales and the fog. They had seen coasters, fishermen, yachts — even the *Silver Shallis* came in for comment. They had worked in the woods and travelled extensively. The rain continued, the fog hung over the hills, the harbor was quiet and gray, and the afternoon passed quickly.

However, Mary came in to point out that we were neglecting our guests. They had taken a walk down the road and out along a path over the cliffs, but they had pretty well exhausted the delights of walking in the rain. Anyone who has flown with The Royal Flying Corps deserves to be warm and dry whenever he wants to be. We returned aboard.

On the way, we rowed under the stern of a chunky little Crocker ketch which the year before had beaten *Eastward* soundly on a long pull to windward. Ollie Gates, professor of geology and a valued contributor to the *Guide*, hailed us and invited us aboard.

His cabin, once we disposed of our oil clothes, was simple and uncluttered. He and his wife lived aboard while he was engaged on a geological survey for the State of Maine. He knows the coast thoroughly. He and I worked for the same boys' camp before the war, each taking parties of campers on short cruises. He told us of George Hoague, a former teacher at Belmont Hill, who had a fine schooner in which he sailed parties of boys. One black night, running down the Nova Scotia coast before a strong breeze, Ollie was sent out on the bowsprit to tie up a jib. He saw breakers close ahead, shouted, and George unflinchingly gybed the schooner all standing, just missing the ledge, and stood off a bit. Then he worked the vessel into a little eel rut of a harbor and anchored, having seen no more than the loom of the land.

It was George's custom to line up his crew of boys on deck every morning, stark naked, and have them dive overboard. When they lined up the next morning, most of the population of the little village was out in punts and dories to admire the visiting schooner. The audience seemed to bother no one.

Another time, coming home from Bermuda with a crew of boys on the same vessel, George lost his rudder. Steering with the sails, he brought the schooner right up Gloucester Harbor, anchored off Rocky Neck and warped her alongside the wharf.

A man like George Hoague has a lot of influence on people he comes near. He was lost at sea on a voyage to the Caribbean long ago, but Ollie emulates his standards of seamanship, his toughness of mind, his readiness to take the calculated risk, his contempt of physical discomfort, and his admiration for a good vessel and a good man. I never knew George myself, but I have known several people who knew him, and afloat or ashore, at sea or in school, he was a strong man.

We could have listened to Ollie longer, but it was clearly time to go. The rain had stopped. The wind had died. The fog still hung over the hills and the air had a wet and weedy low-tide smell about it. We went aboard, torched up, dined luxuriously, finishing off with Christmas fruit cake, and turned in with that plaintive little horn still whining about the fog outside.

14 Our First Foreign Port

I had a restless night, lying awake thinking of the next day's possibilities. The Birkses had expressed an enthusiasm for Grand Manan, a large island lying just off the eastern corner of Maine. Its cliffs converge slowly with the cliffs on the American shore, making a channel about twenty miles wide on the southern end and about eight miles wide off West Quoddy Head. Both shores of the channel are, on the whole, bold water and without shelter except for Bailey's Mistake just below West Quoddy Head. Sardiners bound for Eastport and Lubec from Maine ports run up the Channel on radar without great concern for other traffic. Occasional tankers pass through, lobstermen fish the American shore, and the tide ebbs and flows at rates up to three knots or better on moon tides.

Yet it really isn't perilous in the summertime, for an alert navigator should see the cliffs on either side before he is in serious danger. The twenty-fathom curve runs parallel to the cliffs a safe distance off. A course from Cutler to Northern Head converges slowly with the Canadian shore. There is a powerful fog signal on Long Eddy Point close to the northern corner of the island and another at West Quoddy Head on the American shore. In addition to all that, there are radio direction finder stations at Southwest Head and at

Sardine carrier bound for the factories at Eastport.

West Quoddy. A good man would have to be incredibly unlucky to get lost in Grand Manan Channel.

Yet I lay in my bunk listening to that piping little horn and thinking of heavy, wet fog, of sardiners and tankers, of magnetic disturbances, of three-knot tides, of the tall, dark cliffs, and again of the fog. Just getting out of Cutler Harbor could be confusing, and the entrance to North Head Harbor on the other side might not be easy either. We should be at North Head by eight-thirty in the morning when the tide would turn against us. That meant leaving by five-thirty, possibly before it was properly light. Fog and dark are a bad combination.

There is no sense to this sort of worrying, and no doubt the intrepid mariner of fiction never has such thoughts. Yet summertime sailors who are responsible for a boat and for the happiness and welfare of a crew, sometimes lie awake quite without reason and miserably contemplate unhappy possibilities.

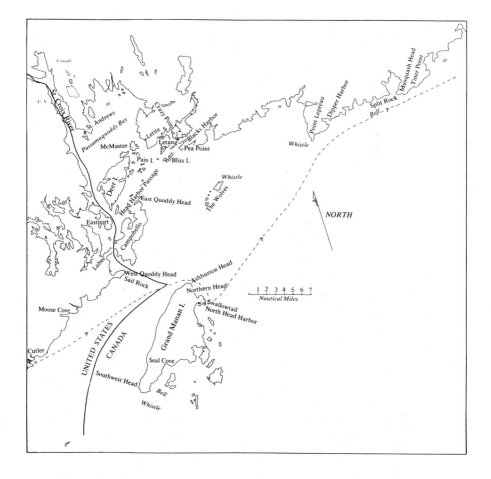

Imagine, then, the relief with which I looked at the early sky through the hatch over my head and saw not the featureless gray of fog but individual clouds against the overcast. It took but two jumps to get into pants, shirt, shoes and jacket. On deck I found it cold and overcast, but the island standing hard and clear in the harbor entrance. The water was iron-gray, stirred by a light northerly air. By the time I had the riding light stowed and the stops off the sails, my crew was on deck and we got under way at once.

Starting before breakfast is ordinarily a poor bet. The first half hour is rather stimulating and adventurous, but the cold, gray dawn over a gray and choppy sea is not good for an empty stomach. It gives one the chills and makes one wonder why he came. However, one takes a fair tide when it is running, for bucking a Fundy tide is a slow and discouraging business.

Outside we found the wind well around to the northeast so we could not fetch Northern Head on the port tack, and a brisk little chop slowed us when we were blocked down hard on the wind. A rain squall drifted down the Channel over the American shore. However, the tide was with us and a streak of blue away in the north suggested that the wind would back westerly. A good breakfast served in the cabin out of the wind improved things a great deal. The rain squall passed. The blue widened to a hard bright band, the wind backed westerly, and we were able to fetch Northern Head at last. In the middle of the Channel we hoisted a Canadian flag to the starboard spreader and became visitors in the Birkses' country instead of their being visitors in ours.

As we approached Northern Head, the tide turned against us, for we were late; but the wind came clear around to the west-southwest. The sun shone in patches and we made our way around the end of the island, finding, as usual, that the situation is not nearly as desperate when one is out in it as one anticipates.

We passed along the cliffs off Ashburton Head, the site of the wreck of the sailing vessel *Lord Ashburton* in a February gale in 1857. One survivor managed to climb the cliffs and get help, but most of her people were lost. As we sailed easily by with a fair wind and a smooth sea, it was only just possible to imagine the black cliffs looming through a screaming snow squall, the breakers white at their base.

The tide, now turning, was making swirls, eddies and whirlpools around us as the tidal stream running down the Bay of Fundy split on the north end of the island. Birds were fishing in the disturbed waters — terns, mackerel gulls, guillemots and a flock of phalaropes — spinning and fluttering on the surface. I remembered one foggy day when we had followed up the shore of Grand Manan from Southwest Head, standing off into the fog and then back to the loom of the cliffs. Rounding Long Eddy and North Head, we found ourselves in a circle of bright sunshine hedged in by the fog to seaward and by the cliffs. In the tide-torn water we hove to for a rest and a lunch after the tension of the morning and found not only the common sea birds but also puffins, seals, and a whale. No doubt the scene below the surface was even more violent than it was above.

Swallowtail Light, an octagonal tower braced against the winter gales with heavy cables, stood sharp against the brilliant sky as we rounded it. With the wind settled cool and dry in the northwest, we ran in for the jetties at North Head Harbor.

After a brief exploration of the two basins, we chose the eastern one, "less traveled by" perhaps, and tied up alongside a heavy sardiner, *Andrew & Deane*.

As soon as we had rounded Swallowtail and opened up the eastern shore of Grand Manan, Mrs. Birks had become increasingly excited. Decades before, she had spent a summer near North Head. As we closed in on the shore, she recognized landmarks, individual cottages and houses, remembered names of people she had known. No sooner did she set foot ashore than she inquired for some of these, found they were still living on the island, and disappeared with Gerald to telephone, visit, and lunch ashore.

Left alongside *Andrew & Deane*, Mary and I cleaned up, stowed sails, and walked up to check in with the Canadian customs and immigration people. The officer, neatly attired and ensconced in a square brick box of a customs house, clean and varnished within, dealt with our simple problem formally and efficiently, then made us welcome unofficially and in a most friendly fashion.

It is always stirring to visit a foreign country, even if it is only eight miles from Maine. The buoys are different. The houses seem different, at least we look at them differently. The Canadian flag, the great red maple leaf, flies over the customs house, at the stern of the ferry, and from our starboard spreader. Our American flag, so commonplace at home, is now a foreign flag. Even the wharves are different, built of huge, squared, tar-soaked timbers, and filled inside with rocks. The boats, great heavy double-ended carriers and 'Scotia boats with high bows and flat waists, replace the sharp Jonesport boats of Maine. Even the people are different. They are no more or less friendly than in Maine, but they talk with a different accent and seem more rooted to Grand Manan than Maine men are to Monhegan or Massachusetts men to Nantucket.

As we were looking across the harbor to *Eastward* lying snugly alongside the carrier, her skipper, Rupert Griffin, hailed us from a car, inviting us to ride to Seal Cove with him on an errand. This was better than lunch, so we drove with him down the east shore of the island. It is low land, rising gently from broad flats to the tar road. On the west side of the road, generally, are the houses, the older ones low-eaved, snug, and close to the highway. Around them are fields, now growing up to spruce and larch but bright with flowers. The few harbors are shoal at low water or dry out altogether and are protected by government wharves, which serve as breakwaters and behind which vessels can lie afloat. There are no really snug, protected anchorages, so the island is little frequented by yachts.

The principal business of Grand Manan is fish. The eastern shore is studded with weirs, some still fishing but many abandoned. A weir is a primitively simple and surprisingly effective method of catching fish. It is simply a brush fence extending out from the shore to a circular enclosure with the lip turned in. The fish follow the fence into the enclosure and continue round and round inside it. Sometimes another leader will extend offshore from the pocket as well as inshore and sometimes there is an inner pocket, too, in which fish can be held.

Fishing a weir is hard work for the fishermen but a grand sight for a spectator. A weir boat loaded with seine is towed into the pocket and the net dropped like a curtain around the sides so the bottom of the net, weighted with iron rings, lies on the mud. The net is then pursed up by hauling on a line through the rings; and if there are fish in the net, the fun begins. A pumper and a carrier are called by radio and the gulls by some more mysterious means. The net is "dried in" to the weir boat, hauled in slowly, hand over hand, forcing the fish into an ever-contracting bag. At first, standing on the carrier or balanced like a gull on a weir pole, you see no more than an occasional silver flash, but as the net comes in, the flashes become more frequent and then the surface fizzes as the fish tail all at once. The pumper drops a black hose a foot in diameter into the net and Hoovers the fish up to a screen which scales them and then skids them down a chute into the carrier's hold.

That is the mechanics of weir fishing but the mere mechanics fail to convey the excitement of the scene. The water sizzles with fish, the men drying in the net heave away at it and exchange cheerful remarks. Fish flip and snip on the screen, water rushes through, a haze of scales and spray fills the air. The radio goes full blast with fisherman talk from the factory and other weirs and seiners. Men in rubber boots, all blue and silver with scales, haul bushel baskets of scales away and replace them with empties. The skipper of the carrier and the owner of the weir watch the fish slide still flipping into the hold, occasionally opening up one with expert thumb to be sure the "feed is out of them." Another with a coal shovel spreads salt on the fish in the hold. The deck is alive with flipping silver herring and an occasional mackerel, dogfish, skate or flounder. Still the radio blasts, the pump rumbles, the water and scales fly, the gulls dip and scream over the net, and everyone is making money. At last the carrier departs, her hold full and deck swimming with fish, the weir boat is towed off, and even the gulls calm down and sit contemplatively on the weir stakes, always facing the wind.

In the winter and spring Grand Manan fishermen go lobstering. This is brutal work in the cold weather and requires the best in boat and gear. The vessels are usually over forty feet long, of the type called in Maine "Scotia boats." Many are built in Meteghan and Wedgeport and along the Fundy shore of Nova Scotia. They are sharp and very high forward with a raised deck and a house above it to protect the helmsman and the men working aft in the low waist. They have a heavy winch geared to the engine and hauling over a davit, for traps are set in as much as thirty fathoms in the winter. An electronic depth sounder, a two-way radio and often a radar are standard equipment. Traps are set in strings of four or five or six or more and are baited with herring, redfish, or whatever offers.

Again, no mechanical description of method conveys any idea of what winter lobstering is like in the rough, confused waters to the east and south of the island where unmarked ledges break heavily, where the fog or snow shuts down, and where in the early dusk of a dark and dirty winter day a man feels a long way from home.

There is some dragging for cod, pollock and halibut in the summer and still a few people go handlining among the Murr Ledges and off the Bulkhead Rip where the water shoals from thirty fathoms to half tide rocks in an underwater cliff. The ebb tide running over this makes such a disturbance that a small boat, even without any sea running, can find it perilous going indeed.

Once on an earlier visit we tied up alongside a diver's boat at Seal Cove. His main business was to remove rocks from inside weirs so the seines would not get torn up, but when not so employed he dove on wrecks to seek salvage. He would get word of the general location from draggers or lobstermen who had had gear wound up in the wreck. Then with a metal-detector he found the vessel, anchored over it, and dove for what he could salvage. One vessel loaded with copper rods was nearly as good as a gold mine.

Mr. Griffin, our guide today, ran a carrier, but her engine was out and he had no pressing business until a new one arrived so we toured the island. At Seal Cove we visited with the customs officer, Mr. Macaulay, who had been of great help with the *Guide*.

Then we investigated a smoke house. These are small barns with dirt floors, shuttered windows, and a hole in the roof along the ridge. This hole is covered with a little extra roof raised about a foot over the peak to keep the rain out. Herring are salted for about a week, strung on sticks through mouth and gills, and hung on racks over driftwood fires built on the floor. A smokehouse in operation leaks smoke under the roof and around cracks in the shutters and gives an aromatic flavor to the whole day; a combination of driftwood, salt and fish makes something which is far more magical than any one of its parts.

When the fish are cured to a strong golden red, they are "stripped." With a few quick strokes of a sharp knife, back fin and belly are cut off and head removed. The fish is wiggled as if it were swimming to loosen skin and bone from the flesh. With two quick pulls the sides of meat are stripped from the skin, and the backbone is peeled out. Fillets of clear, dark-brown meat are packed in twelve-pound wooden boxes and eventually turn up in supermarkets between tired haddock and blocks of frozen codfish. And the magic aroma remains.

On the way back to North Head we stopped at the museum. This was financed largely by the provincial government on the occasion of the recent tercentenary celebration. In front of the simple clapboard building is the main yard of a wrecked vessel, a huge spar fully eighteen inches in diameter and longer than the building. Inside, the main floor is largely occupied by a collection of stuffed birds, collected on the island by the late Mr. Moses. The fishermen knew of his interest in birds and used to bring him unusual specimens that they had collected offshore. To his surprise he received one day a present of an albatross, a bird almost never seen in northern waters. The National Geographic Society heard of it and eagerly sought to purchase it. Mr. Moses reluctantly agreed to sell it if the Society would arrange for him to go on an African safari. He joined a Rockefeller big game expedition as a taxidermist. One evening, far from the Fundy fogs, perhaps feeling a little homesick, he told the Rockefellers that he felt depressed to see so much money being spent in slaughtering African animals when other creatures, particularly eider ducks, were nearing extinction in New Brunswick for lack of refuges. When the expedition returned, Mr. Rockefeller bought Kent Islands and gave them to Bowdoin College as a sanctuary and research center. Bowdoin still owns them and regularly conducts surveys there on eiders, terns, petrels and other offshore birds.

Also in the museum are relics from wrecked vessels and a collection of handmade tools used by carpenters, riggers, blacksmiths and ship-builders in earlier days on the island. In the basement is a geological model of the island and various exhibits showing that the low eastern part is of very ancient rock and the western cliffs are of more recent volcanic origin, blasted molten out of the interior of the planet, cool-ed and subsequently eroded. The brittle crystalline structure breaks off in great blocks and slivers, forming the lowering western cliffs.

Back aboard, we inspected *Andrew & Deane* with Mr. Griffin and admired the simple, rugged construction of the vessel. A trip ashore for groceries, an alarm clock, and gas involved a march along the hot tar road with a full five-gallon can, but we didn't have to march far. A passing motorist picked us up and joined us in the cockpit for a beer. He was the second engineer on the ferry, then on a week's vacation, and cheered the passing moments with recollection.

At last the Birkses returned, delighted with the island and the old friends they had relocated. We turned in, anticipating an early start to catch the flood tide up the Bay to Saint John.

15 Fair Tide to Saint John

With the sky beginning to show the dawn, I woke to sounds of voices, motors starting, roaring, and settling back to idle. It was close to five o'clock, Atlantic time, and the tide was to begin flooding at five-twenty.

By the time we were dressed, the lights on the wharf had paled and the last stars had faded. In the shadow of the wharf looming black and damp as high as our spreaders we cast off from *Andrew & Deane*, cautiously backed out under power, and nosed out between the jetties. A brisk westerly swept cold and dry off the island. Mary took the wheel and shut off the engine while I set the mainsail, staysail and jib. Off Swallowtail we squared away for Lepreau on a course of northeast a half east with the wind well astern and fresh. About this time the Birkses appeared on deck and we took time to watch the sunrise. The sky was very clear, the zenith a hard, deep blue. As the sun broke above the horizon, the level light sparkled the wavelets raised by the offshore wind, making acres of brilliant winking jewels against the black water. Homer must have seen the same colors and felt the same exhilaration when he wrote of the "wine dark sea." The same level light brightened the cliffs against the dark western sky, gleaming on the ridges brilliantly and casting black shadows behind. In five minutes the sun had risen enough to create daytime and it was just another early morning. Magic moments come unannounced and are gone before they are understood.

The sun warmed us, assisted by coffee and the best of breakfasts. With a fair wind, a clear horizon and just enough of a chop to remind us we were at sea, we let her go for Lepreau, still too far away to pick out from the dim blue line of the New Brunswick coast.

We washed up and then settled down for a day at sea — very relaxing in clear weather. The navigation requires only occasional attention. One can write his journal, read, write cards to distant friends, engage in pleasant conversation, or just sit on the afterdeck and watch the boat go. King Solomon found four things too wonderful for him. Of them all, the way of a ship in the midst of the sea is the most wonderful. There is a rhythm to her progress, not a really regular monotonous rhythm but a swinging surge, a rush and a glide, a rising to look over the sea ahead and a settling into the trough. And over it all the wind blows, the sun shines, the sails fill strong and hard, then ease a little as she rolls, and harden again. The peapod painter under my hand came hard taut, slacked a little, pulled again and squeaked hard on the quarter bitt. Euphoria gave way to concern, for the following sea was getting shorter and steeper. Yet it was not as big as the sea off Mt. Desert Rock had been, and the peapod was not behaving badly.

Then, I noticed tide swirls like those we had seen off North Head the day before and the seas rose in sharp little peaks, all bobbly rather than long and even. Possibly the tide running up Grand Manan Channel was meeting the main flow up the Bay of Fundy east of the island.

Whatever the source of the rip, the peapod began suffering. She was being yanked along like a little boy whose mother is running for a bus, and at the same time she was being pushed from behind and slapped sideways by the short irregular chop. She caught a wave under her stern, charged forward and off to starboard while her painter, pulling at a wide angle, tipped her to port as her bow dug into the trough before her and scooped up a pailful of water. While

I was below doing a little arithmetic on the edge of the chart, Gerald and Mary called together.

"She's tipped over."

As I came up the companionway, I could see the painter straining hard over our stern to the peapod's red bottom just awash. I rolled the wheel down to luff, expecting any instant to see the line part or the ringbolt pull out of the peapod's bow, but the gear held. However, with the pull on her stern, *Eastward* did not come to the wind with her usual swoop. Mary got the jib in and slowly we came to the wind enough to shake the mainsail and lose headway.

We hauled the peapod alongside to windward, hooked into the far gunnel with the boathook, and rolled her over. The oars were still under the seats and she would have floated with her gunnels out if it hadn't been so rough. We sloshed a good deal of water out, bailed some more with a bucket, and then wearing a safety harness and lifeline, I got into her and bailed her dry. The worst of it was the way she banged alongside; perhaps we ought to have had her to leeward, but hove to, *Eastward* drifts sideways and we have found she tramples a boat to leeward. We fended off as best we could and then tied our two dock lines, about eight fathoms of seven-sixteenths dacron, to the new eyebolt in the stern and went on our way. The peapod fell in astern docilely and followed us all the way to Saint John without a yaw. She did dig in her heels and haul back hard on the painter, but she came and she kept dry.

About nine o'clock, having been delayed by the bailing, we were up to Lepreau. There stood the striped lighthouse on its rocky point, the tide rip clearly visible and the whistle outside it tooting in short gasps in the chop. Many are the yachtsmen who have been to Saint John and never seen Lepreau, for the fog factory where the thickest, wettest, and most persistent fogs are concocted is in the immediate neighborhood. We took a long look from too far away to photograph the scene and bore away east by north for Split Rock bell.

This was a good sail before the same brave west wind, backing slowly into the west-southwest. The tide rushed us up the shore, a lone-

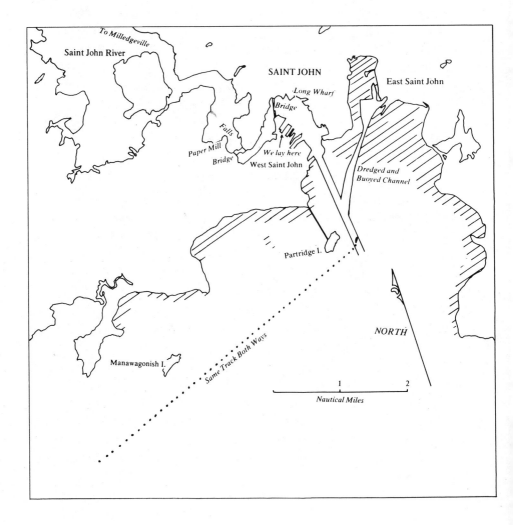

some and nearly deserted coast. Dark cliffs were backed by forests of spruce, alder and larch, rising slowly to rounded hills. We saw breaks in the cliffs at Dipper and Chance with a few fields and a scattering of houses. We saw no boats except for a Canadian buoy-tender hammering along inshore of us. For the most part the shore was as barren as when Champlain had found it. Of course he did not have Split Rock bell to go by, but we never saw it either, although we must have been no great distance from it and Mary nearly missed her lunch in her eagerness to find it. Ahead we saw Mahoganisk and Partridge Island, however; so we left the bell behind us and by one-thirty were up to the entrance of the Saint John River.

Just above Saint John Harbor in the river are the famous Reversing Falls. The river is obstructed by a ledge at a narrow place. When the tide in the harbor is low, the river rushes violently down over the ledge into the harbor. However, with the tide in the harbor twenty-five feet higher, the tide rushes just as violently over the ledge into the river. At the four times a day when the tide comes just to the level of the river, a few minutes of slack water prevail when the alert navigator can pass the falls safely and get into the calm upper river. This was to happen at one-fifty, so, as we rounded Partridge Island before the increasing southerly, we knew we had only twenty minutes to make it.

Up the harbor we rushed under a press of sail. Two big steamers came down on the slack water, planning no doubt to use the ebb tide down the Bay. They moved quietly and very rapidly, their huge size making the roll of foam under their bows look deceptively small. In a few minutes they were hull down on their way. Two others lay at anchor in the mouth of the river, one affecting a clipper bow, keen and graceful.

We charged up the harbor by Partridge Island, luffed to take in the topsail, and found ourselves in the city. From open ocean, bare cliffs, uninhabited woods, we were suddenly sailing over murky waters toward smoke, wharves and tall buildings. To port were long wharves with great derricks for loading containers; to starboard were wharves backed with office buildings.

In a hurry to get to the falls before the ebb began to run too hard, we took in sail. The long day's rush and roll before the wind dropped to a dull and steady putting under the engine. Ahead of us the "new bridge" arched over the river, the water running fast and smoothly under it. We could just gain on it at six knots so knew that the falls would be impossible. There was nothing for it but to lie over in Saint John.

16 Saint John

Saint John and Halifax are Canada's two principal Atlantic ports not closed by ice in winter. Consequently, commerce from all of Canada flows out through Saint John Harbor and products of the world are brought in. Activity on this scale leaves no place for a thirty-two-foot living antique with four pleasure-seekers aboard.

Unable to get up the falls in the afternoon, we ran back with the tide and sought a place to tie up. Sheer concrete walls confronted us, dirty and inhospitable. The Canadian Coast Guard people shouted to us to try Long Wharf. Here was a canyon lined by a concrete cliff as high as our spreaders on one side and by a steep bank of mud, dirt and rotting piles on the other. At the head of this *cul-de-sac* was a landing stage floating in a sea of weed, driftwood, and garbage carried in by the recent flood tide and the southwest wind. A power cruiser, *Lassie*, lay at one end of the float and the open side was used by a party-boat, just then out on tour. One man, staring incuriously at the mass of gurry undulating around the float, suggested we tie to the fenders lying against the concrete wall.

These were logs the size of telephone poles with half a dozen old tires on each end. A chain led from the top of the wall down through holes on each end of the pole so the affair could rise and fall with the tide. Tying to the chain was no good, for the knot would soon be too high to reach and later would disappear fathoms deep. Gerald and I stood on the unstable log and tried to find ways to make a line fast, but the tires were too close together, the log was too big to pass the line under, the whole concern was dirty, and a surge made into the dock which would make lying there uncomfortable anyway. The only way ashore was to row through the garbage-floe to the float, and the city behind it seemed most unattractive.

We fled the place and explored the west side of the harbor. Here was another canyon lined with concrete, but into this one the sun shone and the wash did not penetrate. Best of all, a barge lay alongside one wharf with its deck not more than four and half feet higher than ours and well supplied with cleats and bollards. It was nearly quitting time Friday afternoon, but several members of the crew took our lines, urged us to lie alongside, cautioned us about open manholes in the barge, hauled the barge in so she lay close to the ladder on the wharf, and did everything possible to make us welcome. It was a barge used to carry dredgings, with a bottom that opened to drop its cargo at sea. It was rusty and dusty and no place for a yacht, but it was just what we needed. No ship was due until Monday and the barge would be where she was over the weekend.

Welcome as this sanctuary was, it had drawbacks as a place to spend the night. Perhaps as a protest against the general unattractiveness of the neighborhood, Mrs. Birks suggested that we go ashore to tea. She put on a handsome skirt and prepared to be our hostess. However, she found climbing the four-foot rusty steel side of the barge rather a challenge. The only other way to get ashore was to row to a flight of concrete steps at the head of the dock. They were dirty and slippery and protected by an equally dirty iron rail. The harbor water flooded over the bottom step and withdrew to leave it dripping. One had to step quickly on the slippery concrete and then to the step above or find the water ankle-deep. Nevertheless, showing resolution worthy of one who has moved among the world's most forbidding mountains, she mounted those nasty steps unsullied in character and dignity if not in clothes. Gerald and Mary followed her. I tied the peapod to a dredge, and as I was about to climb the

Eastward *alongside a dredging barge in a berth for container ships at West Saint John.*

dirty ladder, the dredge operator on the wharf, just leaving for home, dropped me his gloves so I wouldn't get my hands dirty. Now that is real thoughtfulness and I said so when I handed back the gloves on top of the wharf.

West Saint John may boast a tea shop, but we did not see it. The boss stevedore, on his way home, gave us a ride uptown and left us between a laundromat and a supermarket, both of which we badly needed. Mary and I got the laundry started and moved to the supermarket. As we were buying a bit of steak for four, the Birkses returned to say that they had decided to leave us. I could not blame them; sleeping aboard *Eastward* as she lay alongside a barge in the midst of a smoky city is scarcely what anyone would do for pleasure. Had we not missed the tide at the falls, we could have spent the evening in the peace and beauty of the upper river. However, the sun, which in rising had quickened the sea and glorified the cliffs of

Grand Manan, in setting would do the best it could with a mustard-colored grain elevator and a container wharf crowded with truck bodies. It had been a good cruise. We called a taxi, set their gear ashore, and bade them Godspeed. They were both people of good spirit.

When we got back aboard, we found astern the power cruiser *Lassie* in command of Lloyd Galbraith. He asked if we were going up the falls that night.

"No," I said. "It will not be slack water until nine and I don't want to do it in the dark."

"It isn't dark at nine," he observed.

I had forgotten we were on Atlantic Daylight Time, one hour ahead of Eastern Daylight Time, and darkness would come later.

"I'll be glad to pilot you up; and once by the falls, it is sheer rock walls on both sides to Milledgeville. No problem." It seemed like a civilized move to make.

After supper, a yawl, *Onrust*, from Connecticut, came chugging in and rafted alongside. She had been in L'Etang the night before, had gotten a late start, and had bucked the tide under power for the last ten miles of the run.

When we introduced ourselves and they discovered that the author of the *Guide* was alongside, they rushed to get their book and I was grossly flattered to autograph it for them. This sort of thing tends to inflate the author's opinion of his own infallibility to the bursting point. Fortunately, circumstances frequently arise to prevent any serious catastrophe.

For example, one summer evening about supper time we were running up the St. George River heading for Pleasant Point Gut. I had never been there before, but the chart seemed clear. Mary turned to the relevant paragraphs from the *Guide*, written by a reliable friend. "There are extensive flats behind Flea Island," she read. We got safely in among the anchored lobster boats, I went forward to handle halyards and anchor, and she took the wheel. I motioned her to round up in a clear space on the edge of the fleet. She rolled the wheel down, and *very* slowly *Eastward* turned toward the wind and gently stopped, her keel deeply embedded in the extensive flats behind Flea Island. We had about two hours to wait until low water and then another two or three until the tide would come enough to float us. We did not lack for visitors, who explained that the *Guide* was explicit on the matter of the flats and urged me to get a copy.

Again on the occasion of our first visit to Saint John our humility was liberally increased. Because we had never made the trip, I had relied heavily upon Messrs. Robert Love and Alan Bemis as well as on numerous other correspondents for the account of the run from Passamaquoddy Bay and of the voyage up the Saint John River. We left Head Harbor, Campobello, with a large Cruising Club of America fleet. There was no wind and the fog was thick. Our speed under power was a mere five knots, so in a few minutes we had lost the fleet utterly. We made the whistle on The Wolves all right and after some hunting we found the whistle off Lepreau in the fog. Thence we ran for Split Rock bell and made that very well, too. With only ten miles to go and time to spare, we were getting a bit complacent when suddenly we heard a tremendous blast and grunt from a diaphone. A quick look at the chart showed no purple dot indicating a lighthouse in the vicinity except Musquash, and that had only a bell. We stopped the engine to listen, hoping we would not hear the rushing bow wave of a great steamer, although I had never heard of putting a diaphone on a boat of any kind. It could not be Partridge Island unless the current far exceeded our expectations. It was shockingly loud, shockingly close, and utterly inexplicable. Then we heard Partridge Island very faintly in the distance and ran for it, ignoring the recurrent blasts as they were left ever farther astern.

We broke out of the fog into Saint John Harbor in time to see the fleet forming in line ahead for the trip up the falls. We fell in, went up in good order, anchored triumphantly at Milledgeville, and went ashore to call home. Waiting on the yacht club porch in merciful darkness we heard two Cruising Club members talking of the day's run.

"What was that diaphone just this side of Split Rock? It nearly scared us out of our shirts."

"Oh, that's Tiner Point. Don't worry about it. It's a horn without any lighthouse. It's all explained in Duncan's book."

About once a year something happens to keep us reasonably deflated. It may be a grounding, the confusion of a name, a letter pointing out that Bucks Harbor is on the *west* end of Eggemoggin Reach, not the east end, or a visit from a wrathful resident of a retired coastal settlement of which I had written in the spirit of Samuel Johnson: "There is no store, no post office, no telephone, nothing but the road out." Last summer within ten days I received two letters, one praising in passionate prose a restaurant of which the *Guide* had spoken well and another damning it as expensive and second-rate at best.

Just before sunset, led by *Lassie*, we got under way and motored up to the falls. The current was still running down hard, sweeping around the corner under the bridge. What we could see didn't look too frightful, and as the tide in the harbor rose, the current would gradually slacken. *Lassie* had power enough to buck the current but offered to wait if we wanted to. Assured that if the current was too strong, we would just be swept back to try again, we rammed the throttle open, swept out of the eddy in which we had been waiting, and found that, although we were clearly going up hill, we could gain slowly.

Right at the pitch of this exciting piece of piloting stands a paper mill. It is an unlovely block of a building, brightly illuminated in the fading light, squirting jets of steam and foul-smelling effluvia, growling and grinding. We hung over close to this thing to keep out of the "pot," a place of eddies, whirls, and boils, which sucks down four-foot pulp logs and shoots them up again with force sufficient to hole a plank or bend a propeller. Once by the mill, the pot, and two little islands above, we motored on in calm water following *Lassie*'s stern light between hundred-foot walls of sheer rock to a quiet anchorage off the Royal Kennebecasis Yacht Club at Milledgeville.

17 Freshwater Interlude

We were dimly aware of rain squalls in the night, but the anchorage was protected and there was no apparent need to slop about barefooted on deck so we just let it rain.

It is possible to get tired on a cruise, so tired that it ceases to be a great deal of fun. I don't mean the kind of exhaustion that hits the ocean racer or the offshore sailor making a passage in a great gale. He may be pushed close to the edge of human endurance, and there is a pleasure in being tough enough to take what you have to take and to win through. I mean just being tired enough so the enthusiasm for something new is dulled, so the enjoyment of sea and sky is tarnished as with a high cirrus on a bright day. Too many long days in a row, too much squinting in bright sun or peering through fog, or heavy wind or rough water can spoil a cruise. Heavy drinking and late nights will do it, too. It is the responsibility of the skipper so to order things that his crew is not only safe but happy. Enough rest, enough exercise, enough variety, and food at reasonably regular and frequent intervals will make all the difference between an endurance grind and an experience delightful to remember.

The time had come for us to slow down. Anyway, it was blowing briskly from the southwest, overcast, squally, and warm. Thunderstorms slammed and grumbled about in the hills and the fresh-water chop sloshed down the cove. We took our time with breakfast, not finishing until after eight-thirty. Then we became aware of a sloop near by. Gerry Peer in *Aronta* of the Royal Kennebecasis Yacht Club came alongside. He was just starting up river with his family and characteristically had stopped to inquire whether the visitors from the States needed anything. As he had helped us generously with the *Guide*, we were delighted to meet him and to be able to give him a copy of the book. We visited *Aronta* briefly and he left for his camp on Kennebecasis Island and a sail up the river.

After a leisurely trip ashore and an encounter with the telephone, we returned aboard with the idea of going up the river, too. The rain had stopped but the wind had increased to a good strong three-lowers breeze — perhaps 20-25 knots. We got under way, sailed to and fro in Kennebecasis Bay, passed east of the island and hardened up for the two-mile beat down to Lands End. It was a real breeze with more in the puffs and a chop that threw spray at us. We would have been more comfortable with a single reef. We slammed away at it for a mile, but somehow it seemed like hard work and not much fun. Such a sail is ordinarily great sport and such a breeze is not to be wasted, but we were tired. I felt a bit guilty in wasting the chance, but we tucked into a quiet cove in Kennebecasis Island and spent the afternoon at leisurely pursuits — Mary in reading, drawing, and nursing a headache, I in sewing up the torn staysail and doing various small rigging jobs. A swim in the warm tea-like water, a good supper and a good long night's sleep improved the prospects of the cruise enormously.

By morning the breeze had blown itself out and the weather seemed exhausted — overcast, calm with only a flicker of air on the still water. A sloop which had anchored outside us after dark got under way and floated gently up the passage. A strange, pink houseboat, which had come in late the afternoon before bearing two avid fishermen, began to show muted signs of life. Breakfast in the cockpit merged into drawing a portrait of a great blue heron fishing in the shoal water. Remembering Gerald Birks's drawing at Roque, I had sense enough to sit still until the job was done.

A little southerly air developed so we got under way, sailed east and north of Kennebecasis Island over calm waters, rounded Lands End and stood up the river. Ahead of us was a local sloop out for a Sunday sail and astern a stumpy little diesel tug towing a long procession of logs chained together. This was an empty pulpwood boom which had carried fodder to the mill at the falls and was going back for another load.

The high shores of the river swept down to fields, little towns, and beaches at the water's edge. On many of these were colored umbrellas, children running about, and people in swimming. Every few miles we came to a ferry crossing. The paved road slowly disappeared into the water. A square-ended scow capable of carrying eight or ten cars lay nosed up to the road on one side with a gangway out. When the ferry was loaded, the engine started up and off she went, hand over hand along a chain stretched across the river. As we approached one, she stopped and stood still, simply holding on by the chain, despite wind and current while we went by.

The atmosphere of the river is so different from the salt water coast of Maine and New Brunswick that it is not surprising people come so far to enjoy it. The fog, which lies so heavily in Saint John, seldom penetrates far up the river; and when it does, it dries up quickly. The water is warm, so warm that we who are used to the 60° water of Maine found it refreshing but not stimulating. It is fresh water, practically, so seems to have a different character from the Atlantic, smelling more of the backwoods and leaf mold than rockweed and clam flats. No tide to speak of changes the shore line from hour to hour. Wharves are little and low, floats almost unused. The high banks shelter the river; seldom is there much of a sea and the chop subsides at once with the wind. Any cove is a good anchorage.

As we eased along up this idyllic stream, the sun began to break through and the wind increased a little. We came upon a small flotilla of yachts in a cove, among which we recognized *Aronta*. An outboard rushed out bearing another very helpful contributor to the *Guide*, Russ McNamara. He, Gerry Peer, Ed Hartshorn and others keep an eye open from their offices in Saint John for visiting yachts entering the harbor and are alert for calls for help in piloting up the falls. Russ had seen us come up the harbor on Friday afternoon and had expected a call. We wished we had called him because he certainly would have enlivened the trip to Milledgeville.

Lots of American yachtsmen talk about going to Saint John and many have been there, but no great number actually make it in any one year, so the hospitality of the Saint John yachting community is not abused and their eagerness is so far undimmed. Besides, anyone who will bring a yacht from Massachusetts or Connecticut through the tortuous channels of Maine and by the tide-scoured, fog-ridden coast of New Brunswick in the sure knowledge that he will probably have to beat all the way back again — such a man will represent the best of New England yachtsmen and will be welcome wherever he goes. So far, not many of the high-charged power cruisers skippered by automobilists afloat have been attracted by the conditions to be found east of Mt. Desert. There is scarcely a single marina east of Schoodic and no place where one can lie alongside and plug in a television set.

As we swung into the cove, made welcome by cheerful waves from all present, Gerry was getting under way. We gybed around Russ's boat, dropped him off, and started to beat back. *Aronta* followed and quickly overhauled us, tack by tack. But when we got around the corner where we could ease sheets and reach down the river, we held even for several miles. *Aronta* was a handsome sight. A photograph would freeze the scene, but an important part of it is the motion — the water white under the bow running aft along the side, the gentle rhythm of the sails, the occasional lift or flutter as she heads a little close to the wind or leans to a puff. It was a lovely sail in lovely company, our pleasure increased by the awareness that *Eastward* was contributing her share to the beauty of the scene.

Together we rounded Lands End again and left the Peers at their mooring. We contemplated an exploration of Kennebecasis Bay and reconsidered in favor of returning to Milledgeville for a walk along the shore. As we were about to start back, a distant cousin of a dory drew up on our lee quarter. She was more like a bateau, flat-bottomed with flared sides and a sharp sheer but lower than a dory, decked over forward with a little house, and painted a vivid blue. In the cockpit stood two men making friendly demonstrations. One, merrily bearded, looked familiar and resolved into Harold Prenatt, music teacher and head of the art department at Belmont Hill, who was to join us on Monday morning for the voyage back to Boothbay. He and his cousin MacAllister urged us to come ashore on Kennebecasis Island for a picnic, a very sound idea. Accordingly, the blue bateau with its two great eyes of portlights in the sides of its house disappeared to windward and we came on the wind. After a good beat, we anchored and the bateau reappeared to take us ashore.

A picnic in New Brunswick bears no relation to sitting on a rock with a peanut butter sandwich. It was held in a little summer camp owned by the MacAllisters and consisted of a superb boiled salmon, home-baked beans, all kinds of auxiliaries like sauces, pickles, salad, bread, and buns, and a great plenty of strong tea. At the end of it all waited strawberry pie. It was like a Thanksgiving picnic.

Afterwards we were given a guided tour around that part of the island. People from Saint John have summer and weekend camps and cottages here which can be kept comfortable from early spring to late fall. Over the years the places have been fixed up very nicely and with a real appreciation for the island. There are open places in the woods and small fields, but there has been no wholesale stripping of the forest cover. The roads are passable dirt roads with grass growing up the middle, very pleasant to walk on. Perhaps a man has laid a flight of stone steps down to his landing beach, but they are unobtrusive. People seem to have given thought to why they came to the island and are consciously protecting it. There is no tremendous economic pressure for "development" here; perhaps this is one place where it can be resisted.

In the dusk we sailed back to Milledgeville, anchored, snugged down, and retreated below as the fog clamped down tight.

Our two days in the Saint John River had been pleasant, restful and easy days among the friendliest and most hospitable people civilization has produced. We turned in, hoping some of them would come west to our part of the coast so we could do our share.

18   The River, the Bay, and Crazy Point

In the morning we motored alongside the wharf to take aboard gasoline, water, ice and groceries. Harold appeared with his duffel bag, not a bit staggered by the small cabin and narrow bunk. It was an entirely new experience to him and he was confronting it with an enthusiasm which effectively subdued his trepidation.

One early spring day I had been working on rowing equipment in the school shop. I came outside to look for early robins and eat my lunch in a sheltered sunny spot. Harold passed by, shared my lunch, and revealed that he had relatives in Saint John. We got to discussing the pleasures of cruising. The combination of the March sun and my pleasant memories led him to suggest that he would like to join us at just the time I was about to invite him.

His cruising experience with us started gently, for there was no wind and it was important to get to the falls at the flood tide slack. That would give us about an hour and a half of head tide in the Bay of Fundy and then a full six hours of fair ebb.

We motored down through the steep gorge, which was created by an earthquake that centuries ago cracked the hill open along a fault line and let the river through. The power lines sweeping across against the sky from cliff top to cliff top seemed so delicate.

At the falls the current was still running down very vigorously, the level of the harbor rising slowly to meet it. We circled about, contemplating tying up at the Saint John Power Boat Club, observing the foul paper mill with all our senses, and watching for the white water to subside. The sun was warm, the breeze very gentle, the proximity of the city a bit depressing. There was no great hurry, for we were sure that with a head tide in the harbor and down the Bay we would move very slowly until it turned. However, as things calmed down for as far ahead as we could see, we moved out into the current and were rushed down. Two yachts passed us bound up against the current as we were swept around the pot, by the paper mill, under the bridge, and into the calm waters below. I expected to face a flood tide but found a strong fair current running. This must have been the fresh water from the river running out over the incoming salt water from the Bay.

We swung around the point under the new bridge and suddenly were swooping down the harbor heading into a great cottony windrow of fog shining white in the sun. I had not expected this. I planned on a head tide to slow us up and give me time to get organized. Things began to happen fast.

Mary took the foghorn and went forward. I gave Harold the wheel and told him to steer for the last visible wharf. I rushed to hang the radar reflector in the rigging lest we be in front of some incoming freighter and hastily laid a course down the line of black buoys on the western side of the channel. As we plunged into the fog, still milky with sun, I realized that Harold, naturally, had never learned to steer by compass. I took the wheel, Mary and I looking for the first buoy. Suddenly we were almost on top of it; it was not quietly anchored on the bosom of the harbor as a buoy should be but was rushing toward us at about four knots with a collar of foam around it — and it was *red*. The tide had skidded us across the channel and any steamer coming up would not pass far from us as we tried to angle back across the channel.

The buoy disappeared astern, we edged back toward the starboard side of the channel, heard the horn on Partridge Island and finally found a black buoy; it, too, was rushing up the harbor. A glimmer of

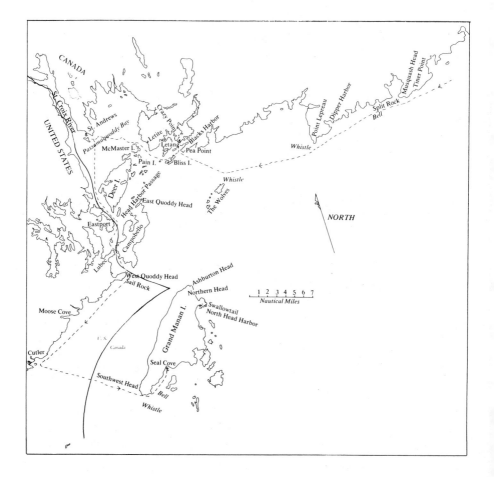

sun showed us Partridge Island wreathed in fog and the last buoy ahead. This one was behaving more as a buoy should with only a ripple running by it. We left it on a course for Split Rock bell ten miles away; and as we established our fog routine for the run, Harold observed, not *really* shaken, "This will be a massive learning experience."

Mary steered, Harold sat on the forward edge of the house with the horn, looking and listening. Navigation in hand, I watched the fathometer and got lunch. The fog pressed in around us. The windless swells rolled in from the south, passed smoothly under us, and disappeared on the starboard quarter as the next ones appeared to port. The cabin clock ticked off the minutes; every twelve minutes a mile through the water. Mary moved the wheel seldom and then only a half a spoke, her eyes on the big diamond of west-southwest on the compass card. *Eastward* rolled easily, swinging her topmast against the fog and chugging steadily on her way.

We had a lunch of sandwiches, bread and cheese, gingerale and an orange. After half an hour, I steered, Mary went forward with the horn, and Harold rested. So it went, rather dully. Half an hour of steering by compass is about enough at a time. The job requires careful concentration to the exclusion of other interests. Long before the half hour is over, the helmsman is seeing compass cards all over the sky every time he looks up. More than half an hour of lookout duty leads to dreaming and inattention induced by the rhythmic pounding of the engine, the gentle motion and the swish of the bow wave.

Mary on the foredeck blew the horn and called to me to keep off to port. Looming dimly, then more clearly, was a big white fisherman with a string of orange floats extending from his stern. It was a salmon fisherman tending a gill net. These curtains of polypropylene mesh are hung in the tide and allowed to drift. The salmon, hunting or playing near the surface, get wound up in the twine. It used to be a very profitable fishery for men from Lepreau to Saint John; but since the Danes discovered where the salmon concentrate off Greenland, the catch has fallen off badly. The Danes complain with some justification that the Canadians catch the salmon when they go up the rivers to spawn and also pollute the spawning areas. The Canadians complain of the unrestricted fishery during the rest of the year. Accordingly both parties have agreed to restrictions and the Canadians are said to be phasing out the Saint John River fishery.

The nets have been a serious menace in past years, however. A vessel crossing one might well share the fate of a salmon and get her propeller wound up. Polypropylene is very tough material to cut and cutting the twine is the only way of getting clear. To go overboard in the Bay of Fundy with a sharp and jagged butcher knife is real punishment, but there is really no alternative. I saw a man cut a net from under the stern of a government boat in Grand Manan and I believe he was the coldest man I ever saw. He did the job and fully earned the warm blankets and hot rum that followed.

Our objective was Split Rock bell off Musquash Head. About fifteen minutes before we should have made it, we stopped the engine. Gradually *Eastward* lost way. The wash under the bow died down. The slap and clink of rigging was all we could hear. Then faintly came the wail of the siren on Musquash Head, the siren which had replaced that diaphone on Tiner Point. The fathometer indicated that we were about the right distance offshore and the compass bearing of the siren, as well as we could estimate it, suggested the buoy was still ahead.

Fifteen minutes later we stopped again. Again the quiet and the recurrent wail of the siren, this time on about the right bearing, but still no bell. The water had shoaled up a little as it should in the neighborhood of the buoy.

On we chugged, pretty much blinded by fog and deafened by the engine, feeling for the bottom with the fathometer.

Again we stopped. This time the bearing of the siren suggested we had passed the buoy. Just then the fog scaled up off the water and there, right astern of us, stood the tall, white bell, perhaps three-quarters of a mile away. We must have passed very close to it and possibly it had lost its clappers for we certainly never heard it and had been listening attentively. However, there was no percentage in fighting a two-knot tide to go back and inspect it so we pressed on for Lepreau.

Gradually the sun dried up the fog and little by little the shore began to show until finally the coast all the way to Lepreau steamed under a warm and hazy summer afternoon. A little air came in almost dead ahead but not enough to beat against, and it was still nearly ten miles to Lepreau and another fifteen or more to any attractive harbor.

Such is the logic when the engine is running and has been running for several hours. One is hypnotized by the routine and the steady pounding of the exhaust. Progress is being made. We are getting where we want to go. We would just slop around if we tried to sail. It is all true, but maybe it would be worth just seeing what would happen. We could get into Dipper Harbor all right. There is a little shelter at The Wolves. If we stayed out all night, in due time morning would come. True, the ebb would set us back up the Bay, but the subsequent flood would be in our favor. With Harold on his first day, however, it didn't seem like the time to try it, so we hammered on by the lighthouse at Lepreau and the whistle outside.

There is a considerable little tide rip just beyond the whistle. If there is any sea running, it can be unpleasant and even dangerous. Coming east in the fog in 1965, we had been set well up into Maces Bay by the flood tide and spent a rough hour bouncing around in that rip looking for the whistle and listening to the blast of the horn on the light to track down the bearing. When you contemplate the run from Passamaquoddy to Saint John by your fireside at home, you don't see yourself standing on the bowsprit holding on by the jibstay, bounced and whirled about in a choking thick fog by a cresting chop, listening with one ear for the whistle and with the other for the fog horn on the light, all the time getting set by the tide in a direction and at a speed which at best you can only guess. As the poet Philip Booth said in *1203*, "The chart is not the sea."

There was no difficulty with whistle, horn, or tide rip this time. Just a bit of a bobble, and then we chugged on for the whistle off

The Wolves, ten miles away. Gradually the afternoon cleared and the breeze came in, even working a bit to the south. When we saw the whistle, we broke through the hypnotism of the engine, shut it off, and made sail for Pea Point. It was a part of the coast none of us had ever seen. There is a big diaphone on the point and a bell buoy outside it to run for if the fog shuts down, and best of all, we could fetch it on the southerly breeze that was now coming in cold and strong off the Bay. Slowly we made sail so that Harold could understand each step and learn gradually the name and function of each line and the pin where it was properly belayed. Then we squared away with sheets just started and a good rail breeze. With the last of the fair tide under us, we rushed up on the land, Pea Point standing up very prominently against the hills behind it.

Suddenly someone turned off the wind. It did not moderate and die out slowly. It just stopped. We slammed about in the confused bobble it left. A puff came from the west, another from the north. The Grand Manan ferry passed on her way from Blacks Harbor to the island. The sun shone more clearly than it had all day as the haze to the westward dried up, but there was nothing for it but to whip up the iron mare again.

Then all at once it was smooth. As we passed the end of Bliss Island and crossed the mouth of Blacks Harbor, the Bay of Fundy feel went out of the day. L'Etang Head and McCann Island with hills a hundred feet high and water a hundred feet deep between them opened the gate to L'Etang Harbor. The sun, level and mellow, lit the cliffs and steeply sloped spruces. Under the shadow of Crazy Point on the western shore we anchored behind a ledge and the quiet flooded us. We did nothing for a bit.

It had been a day of violent changes. From the quiet, sylvan, backwoodsy atmosphere of the Saint John River we had been projected through the falls and through the city into cold, thick fog, ocean steamers and great wharves, then into the routine of fog navigation. This was broken by a grand sail across cold, choppy water in a wind that called for a winter jacket. The day ended in calm water under steep cliffs with the smell of clam flats and spruce. An osprey, high enough to be still in the sunlight, circled over us.

19 The Crew's View
by Harold Prenatt

The sixteenth of July, the day of my introduction to life aboard *Eastward*, presents a series of varied impressions upon recollection. It was a heady day for me, and, of course, a day of new and confusing things to one whose saltwater experience had been miniscule. Two dominant facts bring themselves forward, however, as I recall my first day of cruising and our journey from Saint John southwest to Crazy Point.

The first is the sloop *Eastward* herself, and, inseparable from her, her captain and his cherished and able first mate, Mary. It did not take me long to discover, even in that first day out when three-quarters of our progress was necessarily made under power, that the boat and her crew were one. In the way that a skilled and practiced musician knows his instrument, its foibles, strengths and capabilities, and can bring out the best it has to give, Roger and Mary seemed to know every warp and woof of *Eastward* and made her sing. There was an atmosphere of extremely pleasurable business aboard the sloop, an absence of frills but at the same time a kind of salty elegance, and over all, the pervasive sense that the boat was meant for good cruising.

The captain's patient explanation of nautical basics and his suggestions as to how I could begin to take my place as a crew member ("A little bit more each day. . .you'll get on to it in no time!") began immediately, even as he eased *Eastward* through the Reversing Falls currents at mid-tide, dodging hellish whirlpools right and left. The sun was high and brilliant, the breeze mild, and I could feel my sensations being heightened by the minute.

But then, the fog. . . the great, dense envelope of Fundy mist which sealed up *Eastward* ever so swiftly as she made her way out of Saint John Harbor. This was the second dominant fact of that first day, as I look back on it. Only weeks before, I had made a return ferry trip at night to Woods Hole from Vineyard Haven amid thick fog, but on July sixteenth I sensed the difference between a large, noisy, cargo-carrying ferry with a great blasting horn and a small thirty-two-foot sailing vessel. The image of Mary standing forward, resolutely tooting on the battered hand fog horn every few minutes, the strangely beautiful microscopic condensation of moisture on the fibers of the halyards and my wool jacket. Captain Duncan with one eye on the compass, our vigilant watching for the "nun" off Lepreau whose whistle had minutes before broken into the eerie muffled drone of the engine. . . all of these new and, to me, foreign facts of sailing through fog are recalled now with extraordinary vividness.

As the afternoon wore on, I was asked to take a turn at the forward watch. I easily got the hang of making the fog horn work and soon became accustomed to the slippery forward deck under foot, but within minutes the spray and the thickness had penetrated my clothes and I found myself needing to wipe my spectacles clear every so often in order to see ahead. After a lengthy spell of this, I received an offer of relief by the skipper, but stoically declined.

"Just holler when you want to come aft," he advised. "We're not running a Hell-ship, you know."

The dulling concept of extended sailing through the fog soon precipitated the notion that the next two weeks might prove to be the longest of my life. I meditated on a vision of myself with feet up before a glowing fire, a drink in hand, the stereo playing. I fought discontent.

But gradually, as time passed and we exchanged watches, there was a brightening and a perceptible warming, and then, as quickly and mysteriously as we had gotten into the fog, we were out of it. There was a horizon, a bright sun overhead, and glittering blue swells. Spirits rose, the loathsome engine was squelched, and sails were hoisted. *Eastward* under full sail was something new and fine to me. The vision of glowing fire and mellow stereo, like the fog, vanished as quickly as it had come.

The rest of the day, the last ten miles of coastal sailing through Maces Bay and up past Blacks Harbor, contained further indoctrinations. Campobello and The Wolves were sighted to the southwest, as was the distant hazy outline of Grand Manan. The skipper bit the bullet and permitted me a turn at the wheel, which made me feel as if I had almost arrived. Clothing dried in the bracing breeze. A box of pilot crackers, that eminently suitable seagoing snack, was passed around by Mary. And I unknowingly developed a glorious case of sunburn.

By nine o'clock, after we had dropped anchor in a beautiful little pine-bordered bay above Crazy Point on the L'Etang River, and after clams had been dug, cooked and eaten with some considerable relish, I had become strongly aware of the elemental joys in store for those who go saltwater cruising.

Crazy Point, L'Etang River, New Brunswick. (Prenatt)

20 Art and Literature at Sea

We were awakened at six o'clock by the go-to-work whistle from
Blacks Harbor but luxuriously ignored it to breakfast an hour later
in the cockpit. The wind had come northerly during the night, bringing a transparent quality with it as if after a long day in the library
one had cleaned his glasses and stepped outdoors. We took our
cameras and rowed ashore to photograph what was important about
the day and the place. It is instinctive to preserve and to communicate experiences which have moved us; few but the masters accomplish it with more than limited success.

We take pictures. Yet it is the rare photograph which captures on
paper or screen more than the frozen physical features of the scene.
I have a picture of Pulpit Harbor at sunset, the silhouette of Pulpit
Rock against Penobscot Bay, the Camden Hills and the bright sky.
Those are the principal physical features, but they fail to communicate to a stranger the essence to me of Pulpit Harbor. This essence
is compounded of all my visits from my first trip east with my
father to my most recent visit with my son. As a small boy in short
pants I remember anchoring there, shivering after a run up the bay
before a smoky sou-wester blowing off the cold Gulf of Maine. The
summer after Mary and I were married, homeward bound from running a sailing camp at the head of the bay, we slammed down to

Pulpit Harbor in a hard northwester that worked westerly so we could just fetch the course. The relief with which we anchored in the calm of Minister's Creek is another part of my picture of Pulpit Harbor.

An artist with the camera can do it. Dean Conger of the National Geographic Society was assigned to take his family cruising on *Eastward* and to write an article for *Vacationland, USA*. The article was to be illustrated with photographs. With several cameras he exposed fifty-two boxes of slides in two weeks. Eight of his pictures were finally used in the book. The best of them are communications of the experience in form and color. Unfortunately, though, too many of us are too busy to get the camera out of the bottom of the duffel bag when the magic moment comes and are not sufficiently careful in deciding what to include and what to leave out so that the picture may communicate the experience. How politely we suffer in the dark before the screens of our friends, looking at pictures of people getting into airplanes – breathlessly exciting moments in their lives but, to us who were not present, just another person walking upstairs!

The artist with pencil or brush sometimes does well. It takes more time to draw Petit Manan Light than it does to photograph it, but the man with the pencil can emphasize the slim loneliness of that granite tower in a way a photograph, taken from the safety of deep water, probably cannot catch.

Cruising with our son Bill one summer, Mary and I left him aboard in North Haven while we went ashore. When we returned alongside, I stood up in the peapod and saw propped on a cockpit seat a canvas upon which he was advancing with a brush. A canvas! It was a window into a foggy day, the wind driving the wash from the lee bow, the chop melting into gray, the ghost of a can buoy looming. I stopped him before he killed it with improvements.

Of course the really good professionals do even better. Andrew Wyeth can do more with a white curtain lifting in the breeze from an open window than any words can tell. Winslow Homer and Dwight Shepler could create an experience with line and color and with the implications of a scene. However, their cruises are not our cruises.

If a shipmate is moved to express the day in graphic form, he is certainly to be encouraged even if the dishwater boils away or we miss a tide.

Others use the slippery tool of language to preserve a cruise. Most of us keep log-books, but too many of our most memorable experiences are preserved in laconic pencilled notes which communicate little of what is truly important. This book, of course, is an attempt to communicate what makes a cruise a beautiful part of our lives, to understand and distill the significant detail. The late Frederic Fenger did this superbly in *The Cruise of the Diablesse*. Erskine Childers caught the spirit of a cruise in the Frisian Islands in *The Riddle of the Sands*. Occasionally Joshua Slocum, factual and unimaginative as he appears to be in *Sailing Alone Around the World*, shows that he was moved. At the western entrance to the Strait of Magellan he writes:

> Great piles of granite mountains of bleak and lifeless aspect were now astern; on some of them not even a speck of moss had ever grown. There was an unfinished newness all about the land. On the hill back of Port Tamar a small beacon had been thrown up, showing that some man had been there, but how could one tell but that he had died of loneliness and grief.

At the end of the next paragraph he adds:

> There was a sort of swan, smaller than a Muscovy duck, which might have been brought down with the gun, but in the loneliness of life about the dreary country I found myself in no mood to make one life less. . .

Again, the professionals at their best are hard to beat. Conrad in *The Mirror of the Sea* preserves and shares perceptions with us in language which sharpens our own experience. Kipling wrote a few paragraphs in *Captains Courageous* that put us aboard the schooner.

Masefield, Melville, and Dana, Villiers, Reisenberg, and Forester have transmuted hard, rough experiences into perceptive understanding.

Some do it in poetry, for verse has an impact that few writers of prose achieve. How does one paraphrase Masefield's "A grey mist on the sea's face, and a grey dawn breaking?"

There is something intimate, personal, about poetry; the poet gives himself away, exposes himself undefended to a callous world. Not many care to do it. Philip Booth has a book of Penobscot Bay poems. Robert P. Tristram Coffin wrote a few; but as yet there has arisen no Robert Frost of the New England coast to combine for a wide audience the pictures, the feelings, and the thoughts of fog, squall and summer sunshine.

"Books," says Emerson, "are for the scholar's idle times." He meant that when the rush of inspired expression slows, when Nature no longer fires one to create in her own spirit, the inspirations of another may be welcome. No one can stand too furious a pace. Times of repose are needed. In the quiet of an evening beneath the lamp, on a foggy day, at sea on a long and quiet passage, we often turn to books.

Because a successful cruise is so much a state of mind, what books one brings aboard are of no small importance. We all have our favorite saltwater books, but other books are good, too. I spent a rainy morning in Castine reading Shaw's *Saint Joan*, finishing it as the sun broke through and the wind shifted. The powerful rush down East Penobscot Bay that afternoon was sharpened by Joan's fierce refusal to spend her life in prison away from the beautiful world God had created for her. Her final line, in the context of the play's epilogue, expanded Penobscot Bay beyond Isle au Haut and the sea horizon:

O God that madest this beautiful earth, when will it be ready to receive Thy saints? How long, O Lord, how long?

James Michener, Shakespeare, Herman Melville, Rockwell Kent,

Robert Frost, Ruth Moore, Philip Booth — these are a few of the welcome group that have stood side by side on our bookshelf. But beware of the cynic who cannot see "this brave o'erhanging firmament fretted with golden fire" as more than "a foul and pestilent congregation of vapors." Accurate as his view may be, important as it certainly is to face it, a cruise is not the place. I wish I had read *1984* during a February weekend. To contemplate the consciously planned destruction of a good man's mind and spirit cast a thin and bitter mist over a week in July.

Above all, beware the shoddy, the cheap, the sloppily-written pot-boilers. They leave one frustrated and exhausted with a mindful of dust. Comic books I throw overboard. To the young they are hypnotic. It is easier to read a comic book than it is to do nothing, and it is far less profitable.

One's reading is, of course, a matter of taste; but in surroundings apart from one's ordinary life where sensitivities are sharpened and made memorable, the most sincere work of the best writers is most appreciated. Good writing need not be old-fashioned or difficult, but it should bring to the surface of the reader's mind the best in him and in the world he finds around him. The bookshelf is an important as the galley shelf or the liquor locker. Stock each with equal care.

21 Crazy Point, Blacks Harbor, and Saint Andrews

In a gentle northerly breeze under a clear, warm sky we sailed across to Blacks Harbor to make a necessary telephone call. There was no convenient float, only the steamer wharf towering at low tide some thirty-five feet above the water. The wind was such that we could not bring *Eastward* alongside so Mary rowed ashore in the peapod and climbed the greasy iron rungs of a ladder taller than our house at home while Harold and I sailed up the Harbor and back.

Blacks Harbor presents as foul and violent a contrast as one can easily find. The entrance is between the two great headlands of Pea Point and L'Etang Head. The shores near the entrance are heavily wooded. Further in there are fields and houses near the shore. A buoyed ledge protects the inner harbor.

However, this fairly well-protected and dramatic harbor is dominated at its head by a sardine cannery and a fertilizer plant which sends a plume of foul smoke and a nauseating stench to leeward of its stacks, a stink perceptible for miles. The harbor water is brown rather than blue or green and is so thickly overlaid with a layer of sardine oil that the wind cannot raise a ripple. The heavy sardine carriers, coming in loaded nearly to the scuppers, add a diesel flavor.

Yet it is perhaps unfair to be too critical. I once came out of the lovely museum of the Cape Ann Historical Society to smell a

Gloucester fishstick factory working at forced draught. I commented on it to my guide, a young citizen of Gloucester and a student
of mine.

"Don't knock it," he answered. "That is the smell of money being
made."

Certainly New Brunswick people need the herring industry, farmers
need the fertilizer, and I like the sardines and smoked, canned kippers
that travel a lot farther from Blacks Harbor than does the scent of
its stacks. We have to compromise, but it is interesting to speculate
on the extent to which compromise is necessary.

We picked up Mary, the call complete, then sailed through the
Bliss Islands and around Pain Island with a fair tide and a dying
breeze. Clear sky, bright cold water, dark green woods and gray
rocks seemed so clean and Eden-like that hurry or noise would be
unfortunate.

Gently we rounded Pain Island, picked up a breath of southerly
that gradually increased, and off Mascabin Point, gained enough way
to go through Letite Passage on the very last of the flood tide.

Inside McMaster Island "the blue Passamaquoddy" lived up to its
name. With a fair wind over a smooth sea we came too quickly to
the entrance to St. Andrews Harbor. This we negotiated by carefully
reading the *Guide* and heeding its directions, although there had been
a few changes since our last visit in 1966. We found a guest mooring,
furled sails and cleaned up in what looked like a harbor as big as the
ocean and quite unprotected. As the tide fell, however, Navy Island
and the mainland reached out long sandy arms to encircle and
protect us.

We rowed ashore and found ourselves in a summer resort. A party-
boat lay at the wharf. The main street, well travelled by cars with
the license plates of all the continent, had restaurants, antique stores,
and shops displaying imported woolens and expensive, beautiful
china. We explored these rather tentatively but were attracted more
powerfully to a homey-looking shop selling woolen cloth hand-
loomed in the room above from local wool. We bought enough to
make a skirt, and a friendly Canadian lady helped select yarn with

which to knit a sweater to match. We moved on to a laundromat, a grocery store, and a dentist.

The skipper had been betrayed by a back tooth which had gone completely to pieces in masticating a peanut butter sandwich in Letite Passage. Damage to one's physical machinery on a cruise is unnerving. Who can fix it? What does one do? How does one handle pain, either in oneself or someone else, which may have no prospect of relief for several days? In *The Old Man and the Sea* Hemingway speaks of the old man's feeling betrayed by his cramped left hand. An upset stomach, a sprained ankle or a broken tooth makes one feel that an important part of his equipment has let him down. Fortunately in this case an able and friendly dentist did a major job in a short time and to help the Novocain wear off, the skipper took all hands ashore to a restaurant for dinner in style, a change welcomed with enthusiasm by cook and crew.

22   Saint Andrews to Cutler

In the morning our son Bob joined us after a bus ride which landed him in St. Andrews well past midnight. He was joining us for the pleasure of the trip home and to gain experience in eastern waters.

We made sail on the last of the ebb and floated down Passamaquoddy Bay before a light northerly air. When the tide turned, however, the wind died and progress became a negative number. This situation is one of the reasons for having an engine so we fired up the machine and continued down the bay. We closed the American shore near Kendall Head and suddenly found the flood tide was something to reckon with. We could only just make headway against it. By swinging into the bays between the headlands we got some back set, but at the Dog Island beacon off Eastport we were hit hard. The engine chugged steadily, water curled from the bow. A fine wake stretched astern, but Dog Island beacon hung right abeam. With Bob watching the fathometer, we eased in toward the shore, getting in close enough so it would have taken no George Washington to toss a silver dollar ashore. I could have done it with a dime. In two fathoms of water, almost on the edge of the rockweed, we crept ahead. Once by the island, we hugged the end of Eastport's wharves and were able to continue down the bay.

We had a close look at Eastport and a sad sight it is. The sardine canneries appeared to be closed and deserted. Some of the wharves were in ruins. The post office and weather station, the "Eastport" of "Eastport to the Merrimac River" stood square, stern, and Victorian amid dull wooden buildings. It is easy to see why some people want an oil refinery here — or indeed anything that will give them profitable work.

As we speculated on this project, we turned our backs on Eastport and looked across to Deer Island and Campobello. Here, a mile wide, is a region of the most violent tidal activity around. The main force of the flood tide runs up the eastern shore of Campobello, around East Quoddy Head and southwest through Head Harbor Passage. Off the southern end of Deer Island it makes a hairpin turn and meets another branch of the current coming north through Quoddy Roads and Lubec Narrows. The situation is further confused by the current coming down the St. Croix River, the current flooding through Letite Passage into the upper bay and the vast volume of water in Cobscook Bay. The result is a turbulence on both flood and ebb that passes ordinary credibility. I passed through it once in a forty-foot schooner with ample power. We were swung from side to side, turned halfway around by whirlpools thirty or forty feet wide and three feet deep at the vortex. Great boils burst to the surface, raising a bulge perhaps two feet high off which the vessel slid sideways. Sardiners negotiate this rip in ordinary weather under full power, but in heavy weather at the full flow of the tide it is best left alone. Furthermore, no one knows what conditions prevail twenty, thirty, or forty feet deep. A good skipper, aided by tugs, could perhaps bring a supertanker through Head Harbor Passage. But to bring in several of them each week in fog or storm through a channel with jagged rocky sides only a few hundred yards wide would sooner or later lead to a *Torrey Canyon* disaster that could put a "bathtub ring" around the whole Bay of Fundy and ruin the herring and lobster fisheries for years. Certainly we could understand the Canadian government's reluctance to sanction the use of Head Harbor Passage for vessels which at slow speeds are almost unmanageable and which are longer than the width of the channel.

Yet Eastport is economically in really serious trouble. We wondered whether, in our increasing energy shortage, the power of these tides cannot be made to work for us. President Roosevelt's Quoddy Project, derided in the forties, might save eastern Maine in the seventies if approached with the resources and the ingenuity the nation has mustered for less productive efforts.

None of us are engineers and no doubt we speculated from ignorance, but in the tradition of the town meeting we voted unanimously for an investigation of the possibilities.

The abandoned lighthouse at Mulholland Point in Lubec Narrows on the Canadian side.

We approached the Lubec bridge. This monument to Canadian-American amity, if a friendship so solidly based needs a monument, was constructed over the southerly exit to Passamaquoddy Bay to allow Americans to visit President Roosevelt's summer home and to make easier the transportation of fish from Wilson's Beach to American markets. However, for lofty yachts it raises some interesting problems.

The bridge has a clearance of forty-seven feet at mean high water. By measuring our topsail halyard and the height of the deck above the water and adding a generous foot for the height of the mast above the sheave of the topsail halyard block, we concluded our topmast stood forty-seven feet three inches above the water. The high water slack at Lubec comes about an hour to an hour and a half before the top of the tide — that is, the current is slack while the water is still rising. This led us to believe that if we approached the bridge at slack water, we would have two feet nine inches clearance over our masthead. If we were wrong, the headstay would break and the topmast would come down with it — or the bobstay, bowsprit and topmast would all let go practically simultaneously. If we were late and found the tide running with us under the bridge at close to seven knots, there would be no turning back. Yet mathematics, which is said to be an exact science, told us we were all right.

With one sardiner ahead of us and another behind, we edged up to the bridge and found the tide slack. As the fisherman behind us overtook us, he waved amiably and shouted over the howl of his high-speed diesel what sounded to Mary like "Pretty close" and to me like "Plenty of clearance."

We slid under and, with great relief, shut off the engine and sailed down Quoddy Roads with a light, fair breeze.

We rounded West Quoddy Head with its well-known candy-striped lighthouse, passed outside Sail Rock, the most easterly nubbin of dry land in the United States, and stood down Grand Manan Channel with the beginnings of the ebb tide. The cliffs of Grand Manan stood square and flat-topped to the east. The cliffs of the American shore were closer and more jagged but almost equally inhospitable. The

*West Quoddy Head, the easternmost point in the United
States.   The lighthouse is behind the trees.   The distant
land is Grand Manan.   (Prenatt)*

wind was light and progress slow.   Bob slept.   Mary tried the fish.
She had towed a mackerel lure practically all the way from Bar
Harbor to Saint John and back for a total catch of three mackerel
and those in the first two hours.   But never discouraged, she persevered, and when progress slowed to less than one knot, she tried for
codfish.   Harold steered and sketched; the skipper devoted most of
his attention to rehabilitating the worn jib topsail and the rest of it
to supervising a small tanker bound east outside us and a big schooner
with fore and main topmasts motoring up the American shore against
the tide.

Finally about four-thirty we started the engine off Moose Cove and
motored into Cutler in a flat calm to find ourselves surrounded by
our brethren of the Cruising Club of America.

After two weeks with scarcely a sight of another yacht, we slipped
into the quiet harbor of Cutler to find it vibrant with deep-water

racing and cruising yachts manned by sunburned men in shorts and capable, self-possessed ladies. We slipped in apparently unnoticed, except by Ollie and Jane Gates who came aboard for a beer with us. We became conscious of the sound of people talking all around us, something we had not heard for a long time.

A seaplane appeared overhead, circled and landed on the smooth harbor. The pilot, another member of the Club, was distressed that the restaurant which formerly flourished at Cutler was no more and presently departed for dinner in more civilized climes.

It began to rain just before dark. As I hung the kerosene riding light in the rigging, fisherman style, masthead lights flicked on all over the harbor, canopies were raised over hatches and cockpits, electric lights shone from cabin ports and a wire halyard "tinged" rhythmically against an aluminum mast. The smell of frying steak came downwind from the group of four yachts rafted ahead of us. I went below to our dimly-lit cabin and constructed a hash of canned corned beef and boiled potatoes, at which the crew turned up no noses.

Later that evening we were hailed from on deck and found coming aboard from an inflated rubber doughnut a Belmont Hill colleague, John Hallowell, who had recognized *Eastward* from her pictures. Just back from Nova Scotia and the Halifax Race in a fast little yawl, he shared his experiences with us and no doubt acquired a little of the atmosphere of our cruise.

23 Rendezvous

The rain ended in the night and brought a calm morning too cold for the morning swim. In the tradition of George Hoague, Mary and I usually get over the side. Bob refused to go without a fight, and Harold was eclectic about it, showing a good sense for the anchorages with more moderate temperatures. No doubt diving into cold water is a bad habit which takes years off one's life, but we like it.

As we nursed our coffee mugs in the cockpit, the fleet awoke. People appeared on deck in pajamas and disappeared to return and wash down decks in shorts. Prams with little outboard motors just big enough to stir a drink churned from boat to boat. Some breakfasts were served in cockpits. Conversation became general.

We went ashore and met on the wharf a former colleague who was in desperate need of a set of points for a Universal engine. A vital little spring had broken, without which, in no way, could the machine be induced to run. Mechanics, professional and amateur, had held a clinic on it but so far improvisation had failed and our friend was about to go to Machias to seek points there. It just so happened that *Eastward* had a spare set of points aboard somewhere. A vigorous search in the chaos of the tool box revealed the empty carton. By removing most of the tools and sifting the substratum of nails,

124

screws, and small things that "might come in useful some day," we finally came up with the points. It was with satisfaction that we paddled over to the afflicted vessel.

While we were on the group of yachts rafted together, we visited John Hallowell on *Antelope* and saw a really successful modern yacht. She stands higher out of the water than *Eastward* and is far narrower for her length. Gleaming stainless steel stanchions support double wire life-lines around her deck. Her main boom is short and very light, her mast tall and far aft. Halyards are wire and are set up bar taut by winches, some halyards even running inside the hollow aluminum mast. The decks are wide and clear except for two spinnaker poles lashed in chocks. Every effort is made to achieve strength without weight or wind resistance. There is a highly strung intensity about her on deck which is belied by the brief glance we got below of varnished mahogany, teak, upholstered bunks and an air of gracious living.

John and the skipper, his brother, brought out the chart and showed us how they had brought her through a passage inside of Seal Island in a dungeon of fog with a roaring fair tide, going by compass, RDF, depth finder, and a very accurate log which measures both speed and distance. We marvelled at their nerve and admired their success.

As we returned to *Eastward*, the fleet began to get under way for Seal Cove, Grand Manan. Some motored out and set sail outside, but many set mainsails at anchor, brought great bags of jibs on deck and snapped them to headstays. Rafts broke up, anchors came aboard, and in a very gentle southerly air the fleet moved down the harbor, each vessel flying the Club's white pennant with a blue wave.

Eastward did very well with her huge mainsail and topsail. We even set the jib topsail which had been repaired the day before. Outside, with a fine reaching breeze and every stitch set, the fleet stood across Grand Manan Channel for Southwest Head. Soon more sails showed over the horizon to the southwest as boats which had spent the night on the Maine coast at Roque Island, Cross Island or the Cowyard joined the fleet. At noon we counted twenty sails in sight;

Southwest Head, Grand Manan. The cliffs are over 200 feet high. (Prenatt)

this did not include power yachts or those which had already round-ed Southwest Head.

After two weeks of nearly solitary cruising, it was exciting to see so many fine vessels under sail and to see that, in those ideal condi-tions anyway, *Eastward* stayed with the fleet. *Antelope* and some others of the fast fraternity outran us but we were not left ignomini-ously behind.

As we approached Grand Manan, the cliffs loomed higher and seemed steeper than they had at North Head. Neither Harold nor Bob had been here before, so we ran close in to get the feel of them and to take pictures. As we got within a quarter of a mile, the wind softened and the bobble shook out what wind there was in our sails. We stood off again, awed by the height and by the way the rock broke off in long slivers and blocks to accentuate the steepness.

Here, just north of Southwest Head, William and Lucas Jones drifted ashore one February night in a skiff. They had been raking sea moss off Haycock Harbor on the American side when their outboard quit and a winter northwester carried them across. Their skiff was wrecked at the foot of the cliff and they scrambled to a narrow ledge. Pretty nearly frozen, William made his way up the icy cliff and through hip-deep snow to the light station whence a party set out to rescue his companion. Logically, I suppose, there was little choice, for they never could have survived the night on the ledge. Yet to set out up the cliffs took courage and to keep going must have taken more.

On this sunny afternoon, however, we soon rounded Southwest Head and, with a strong, fair wind, ran with the fleet up to Seal Cove, took in sail, and tied up alongside ex-Commodore Howland Jones's *Silver Heels*, a fine schooner designed by Murray Peterson in the tradition of the coasting schooner as *Eastward* was in the tradition of the Friendship sloop. I felt we belonged together.

Here was such a raft-up as Grand Manan seldom sees. Forty-three of the fastest and finest of East Coast yachts, including winners of famous races, lay side by side, glittering in varnish and stainless steel, made fast to a government wharf soaked in creosote and accustomed to battered Scotia boats and rugged sardiners. All Grand Manan was

The harbor behind the breakwater at Seal Cove, Grand Manan, at about two hours after high water. (Prenatt)

there to see, promenading the wharf and lining the road above, taking pictures side by side with the yachtsmen.

We walked over to the smokehouses we had seen on our last visit and found a room full of silent, white-clad women stripping smoked herring and packing them in twelve-pound boxes. They had no time to talk with us, but from the owner of the operation we bought a box. After taking more pictures, we returned aboard and, taking the box of herring with me, I made a progress through the fleet, distributing a few herring at each stop, for I knew we could not handle twelve pounds. I returned from the pleasant trip and found that I had done not wisely but too well, for the bottom of the box was nearly visible.

At suppertime we got out clean clothes and were conveyed to the Curling Club. The Club engages in intramural curling here, on an artificial rink in the winter, and sends a team to compete ashore. Several times during the winter, meets are held in the Grand Manan

The inner harbor at Seal Cove, Grand Manan. The break-water is just visible in the center, to the right of it are smokehouses. This cove dries out completely at low water. (Prenatt)

Club and are contested with as much spirit but not as much bitterness as are hockey games in Boston.

Here the inhabitants of forty-three yachts and their Grand Manan hosts stood in line for drinks, met old friends and former acquaintances and found new ones. Everyone felt himself in the presence of friends, acted that way, and it was so. Among other people was present Captain McMullen of *Saechwen*, who had crossed from England, cruised on the New England coast, and was on his way back across the Atlantic. His vessel was by the standards of those present a bit battered and considerably under-rigged, but she had a deep-sea look about her that demanded respect.

After an excellent turkey dinner prepared and served by the ladies of Grand Manan, we returned aboard and went to bed, only slightly disturbed by the activities of the million-dollar ghetto in which we floated. Travelling in great fleets and visiting about is a welcome break in a cruise. We see other kinds of yachts, talk with people who have had other experiences — often very interesting or exciting or raucously funny experiences and as different from ours as our boat is from theirs. Sometimes we have chances to contribute something, too, and to astonish some modern types with evidence that old-time, gaff-rigged, wooden vessels can sail. To sit in a boat's cabin in Maine and hear two men arguing from personal experience about how hard the wind blows under Table Mountain or the nature of Iceland's bird population is an opportunity rarely encountered. Yet of fleet cruising we can say as Shakespeare said of honey, "A little more than enough is by much too much."

24 Grand Manan to Roque Island

We awoke to the rattle of the alarm clock, throttled at once lest it arouse the whole raft, and ate breakfast hastily, aware that the tide was running hard to the westward in our favor and that by nine-thirty it would turn against us. On deck about seven-thirty we found the fog packed in solidly all around us in the prevailing calm. The raft was silent, there being nothing much for these eastward-bound mariners to get up for until the tide turned. We wriggled out of the nest, and as we passed the end of the wharf, we were hailed by a departing fisherman.

"Too foggy, Cap. Better go back."

The tone so belied the words that it sounded more like a cheery welcome to a merry day on the water than serious advice.

While I had been watching and listening to the fisherman, the solid wharf and the web of rigging over it had disappeared — completely. *And the compass was cockeyed!* Our course was southwest a quarter west for a bell buoy three and a quarter miles away, but the big triangle at southwest on the compass pointed straight at where the dock had been, about west-northwest. There was no wind, no sound above that of the engine.

We were lost within mere yards of a solid government wharf and a large fleet of yachts. My first panicky reaction was to back the engine, stop all progress, go back to the wharf, and get straightened out. The reverse gear growled and we lay on the slick, still sea completely disoriented – a most unsettling feeling right after breakfast.

A quick exploration revealed no knife carelessly laid down in the binnacle, no light meter or portable radio near the compass, no galvanized bucket or foghorn in the cockpit. The compass had been accurate the day before. It is such a simple mechanism and controlled by such a simple and pervasive force as the earth's magnetic field that the chances of my being wrong were much stronger than the chances of the compass's being radically deflected. So in harmony with reason and contrary to every instinct, I headed southwest-a quarter west on the compass and slowly went ahead toward what I felt to be certain disaster.

Mary watched ahead with radar eyes. Harold called off the depths under us from the sounding machine in the cabin. Bob stood ready for whatever emergency might arise.

A couple of old weir stakes ghosted by. The bottom gradually fell away beneath us. We moved steadily in the middle of our tiny circle of visibility in the choking fog and no disaster befell. On schedule we made the bell, then the whistle off Southwest Head, and set a course for Libby Island over twenty miles away.

Most of the people who suffer disaster are absolutely sure they are right – hence the "uncharted" rock on which so many strike.

The run across to Libby Island is best forgotten. It was rough, tedious, and uninspiring. The fog lay heavily upon us. The sloop rolled, pitched and combined those motions in the confused chop. Unremitting was the steady pounding of the engine. In our wake the peapod followed, obedient and bored. Watches shifted every half hour and nothing whatever happened.

At last, thinking we must be somewhere near Libby Island, we stopped the engine and listened. At once we heard the grunt of the big diaphone about a point to starboard and ten minutes later saw the end of the island looming dimly. The breeze came in southerly so we made sail at once, shut off the pounding engine and headed for the bell buoy off the Brothers.

The world of sound came alive. Over the background of the wash under the bow and aft along the rail we could hear Libby blowing astern. The leach of the mainsail fluttered. The nylon ensign snapped. A tern shrilled nervously. We strained to hear the bell but heard no tinkle or distant clang — just the drip of the fog dew.

In a scale-up at last we saw the bell and a nun, and ran into Roque Island Harbor by Halifax Island where fog and wind together left us becalmed and resting in warm sun, sails motionless, flag hanging slack.

After the long pull under power and the strain of the fog, we enjoyed the certainty of our surroundings, the quiet warmth, the damp smell of weedy rocks and sun on spruce and juniper. The great white beach swept almost half way around our horizon. Mary tried for codfish and no one else did much. Just as we were about to start the engine, the wind came in again and gave us a good beat up the Thorofare into our snug anchorage in the mouth of Bunker's Cove. Here we found company, a long, sharp, black sloop aptly named *Vanitie*, sparkling in gloss paint and varnish. She did not seem out of place, however, for there was a dignity about her, an air of aristocracy, which fitted the island.

For over a century the island has been owned by the Gardner family and has been managed with excellent good taste and sound judgment. They have built several houses on the sheltered northerly side of the island and there maintained dairy cows, big gardens and a hayfield. The rest of the island is wild, criss-crossed by wood roads which serve as fire trails and populated by sheep, deer, pheasants and a wide variety of birds, all of which are protected. In a rainy southeaster years ago I marched the whole length of the island seeking bread for my hungry crew and was most generously supplied by the family from Jonesport then running the farm. The island has a feudal atmosphere about it but entirely without the dark air of oppression and cruelty the word suggests. It is a fragile atmosphere, one which depends on generosity, good taste, the friendly cooperation of owners, residents, and visitors and on financial security acquired elsewhere. The loss of any of these factors would destroy the delicate

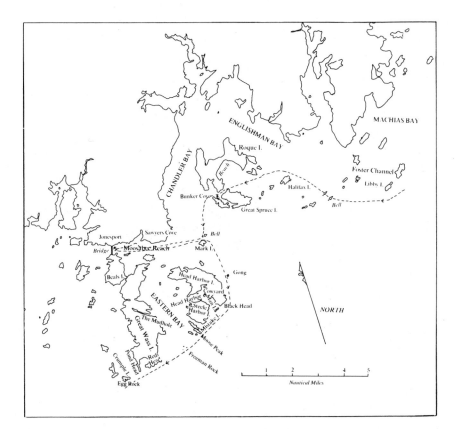

MACHIAS BAY

ENGLISHMAN BAY

Roque I.

CHANDLER BAY

Foster Channel

Bunker Cove

Halifax I.

Libby I.

Great Spruce I.

Bell

Jonesport   Sawyers Cove   Bell

Bridge   Moosabec Reach   Mark I.

Beals I.   Head Harbor I.   Gong

Cow yard

Head Harbor I.   Black Head

Steele
Harbor I.

EASTERN BAY   Mistake I.

The Mudhole   NORTH

Stone Peak

Crumple   Pond Head   Red
Head

Freeman Rock

Egg Rock

1   2   4   5

Nautical Miles

balance and make Roque something very different from what it is today.

The uniformed skipper of *Vanitie*, seeing our un-uniformed mate rowing ashore with a bucket, generously lent her his clam hoe. She returned in an hour with the bucket nearly full. Digging clams, while perhaps not an art, has a definite technique which produces far faster results than digging down a clam hole with a stick of driftwood. The professional digger usually gets his back to the water to take whatever advantage he can of the gentle slope of the flats. Treading near a clam hole, he may get a squirt from one. He spreads his legs wide, bends at the knees to save his back as much as possible. Seizing the hoe in one hand at the upper end of the handle and by the other at the lower end, he drives the tines deep into the mud about eight inches short of the clam holes. Then lifting the end of the handle and shifting his weight aft, he hauls out a clod of mud, sand and pebbles. Next he digs in beyond the clams and tips the clod into the hole. With quick and practiced hand he picks out the clams from the loosened mud and sand and tips another clod into the hole. If there are any clams around, he quickly gets enough for a chowder. However, as a way of harvesting a crop, it is wasteful indeed. Despite his best care, the digger spears some clams on the tines of his hoe. The clams too small to take are disturbed and exposed to their enemies, and the ecology of the flats is disrupted. The State of Maine now requires that diggers be licensed and many towns impose regulations. Some years ago there was a "clam war" between Jonesport and West Jonesport about jurisdiction over certain flats. What used to be the resort of poor families in hard winters now is a regulated source of income. To "strike for the clam flats" used to mean to a Maine man almost what going on relief means today, and in hard years steamed clams and shore greens carried people through rough winters.

With potatoes, onions, salt pork and milk the skipper built a chowder which, assisted by corn bread and a drop of New England rum, was a supper suitable to the surroundings.

25 Digression to Jonesport

The weather stalled as it sometimes does in midsummer. The early morning radio rattled on about an occluded front somewhere in New York State which might not advance eastward because it was blocked by a high pressure area that had lain down exhausted off the coast. What it all meant was light airs and thick fog, maybe burning off in patches or stirred by zephyrs. It meant no "chance along," as the coasters called it, for a beat down Eastern Bay or a long, close reach by Petit Manan and Schoodic.

So the skipper set the clock back an hour to Eastern Daylight Time and crept back into the bag with no dissenting vote from the crew. The fog dew smacked on deck, a gull silently crossed the gray square of the hatch, and nothing at all happened.

Thoroughly awake, in contrast to the crew which was thoroughly asleep, I contemplated the possibilities for the day as a fog shower freckled by. We ought to do something to make the day worthwhile to Bob and Harold. Surely lying indolently at anchor would produce nothing but a bad case of cabin fever. We could march through the soggy woods ashore, battling mosquitoes, to visit with any Gardners who might be at home and maybe dig some more clams or take a ritual swim on the beach. Bob would not go for that program without a fight and Harold would be too polite to refuse. We could whip up the iron horse and motor the forty miles to Mt. Desert and never see a yard of real estate all the way. After the long haul under motor the day before, it was not a very attractive thought. Besides, the next day might be better. In view of our obligations to the U. S. Customs, our need for food, gasoline, and laundry, and the honest commercial nature of the town of Jonesport, I decided to introduce Harold to a Maine town pretty much "unspoiled" by summer people. Once the decision was made, lying a-bed while the fair ebb tide ran under us seemed a serious waste.

The crew displayed no great enthusiasm for moving and no great concern about the tide. They had never seen it pull by Nova Rocks at a generous four knots! But there was no mutiny. They rose up and even tackled fried salt herring for breakfast. I should have soaked it out. It was as salty as Lot's wife and produced at once a great thirst and a repetition of the story of John Blake, a Novascotiaman, as told by the late Captain Edward A. McFarland of New Harbor.

Seems as though John Blake came down from Nova Scotia to go in Gloucester fishing schooners. Now in Nova Scotia they didn't use salt beef in those days. They killed their beef in the late fall, hung it and froze it, and had it all eaten before spring. Well, on the schooner they had salt beef the first day, and John loved it.

"Say, cook, you got any more of that salt beef?" he asked as Cap'n Ed imitated him in a puckered falsetto voice.

"Sure," said the cook. "Help yourself out of that barrel there" — indicating the harness cask. John went for it with his knife and cut out several generous chunks. After he had devoured a pound or two right out of the cask, the salt began to get to him. "Didn't taste salt," he shouted, "but, Christ, it must a ben salt. Pass the water, boys." Ed said they made him drink half a pint of vinegar before they relented and gave him water. Ever since, the expression has been quoted freely with reference to alewives, bacon, and salt spilled in the soup. It certainly fitted the herring.

We cleaned up, got the anchor, and plunged off into the mists for Jonesport. The route was tortuous and marked principally by nun buoys, about which one fisherman remarked, "They're awful damned silent." The sea was smooth, the courses short and most of the landfalls easy, for the tide was about slack. Under a bit of a scale-up, we slid past the wharves of Jonesport to the east side of the bridge, constructed for the convenience of the residents of the town of Beals and the inconvenience of tall yachts. Here we found a commercial fish wharf with gas pumps and a lobster car but no gangway. Accordingly we took a mooring, landed at the car, and laden with laundry bags, climbed the slippery ladder to the wharf. The Maine Publicity Bureau and the Department of Economic Development would have had fits. The planks were greasy with lobster bait and gray with fish scales. Barrels of bait stood about, more or less salted and smelling strong enough to walk on. A window in the fish house was broken. The little "office" near the end of the wharf was tiny, close, and smelled of winter — a dead and stuffy smell in which oil, tar, and tobacco fought for supremacy. The inhabitant, a cheerful man in a red-checked cap who had hailed to offer us a mooring, showed us the way to the Coast Guard station, stores, and laundromat.

The Coast Guard was most hospitable, telephoned the customs office at Eastport for us, and declined to search the vessel for smuggled goods. There used to be a customshouse at Jonesport in years back, but lack of business shut it down.

Jonesport is principally one long street running parallel to the shore of Mooseabec Reach. Just walk far enough and you will see it all. There are sardine canneries, great red buildings that used to employ hundreds of people when the sardine carriers came in loaded to the scuppers and the steam whistle blew. White-clad ladies, their hair tied up in kerchiefs, stood at long tables picking fish off conveyers, snipping them to the exact length of the cans, and packing them at so much per case. Machines squirted measured doses of oil, mustard, or ketchup, sealed up the cans, and delivered them to massive pressure cookers.

Now, with no fish and no price, the whistle never blew.

A man trimmed the edge of his walk with an axe. A boat shop stood silent, the victim of the high price of lumber and the scarcity of lobsters. Jonesport boats, many of them built across the Reach at Beals, have character, a speedy sweep of sheer that identifies them anywhere. They are high, narrow, and sharp forward with a tiny foredeck steeply slanted to their quick sheer, running aft to a low, narrow cockpit and a sawed-off stern. They used to have canvas spray hoods forward to protect the helmsman and a sail on a short mast aft to hold her in the wind. Now they have a low deckhouse and a narrow shelter aft of it. They are powered often with massive automobile engines, exhausting straight up through the house. Jonesport men are competitive. They don't often race, but to see two of these boats, enormously overpowered, throwing wide wings of spray, dragging half of Mooseabec Reach astern in a boiling wake, "trying her out" on the way home is a sporty scene.

At the far end of town we passed the machine shop. A friend of ours, towed in here with his steering gear disabled, found quick, eager, and interested help performed with skill and dispatch. Next the site of a projected marina. It was a scene of great activity, for the State had concluded that a marina would attract business. New piles stood in the mud and shallow water. A small building housed what would become toilets, showers, and laundry machines. A flagpole would be erected, a "yacht club" established, and a steward employed to be of service to yachts in need of fuel, supplies, and the amenities of the shore. Telephones and electric plugs would be provided. But all this would do little to dispel the fog or lift the bridge. It is rough country for motor yachts, for the run from Mt. Desert around Petit Manan is likely to give the high-charged, short-ended, shoal-draft powerboat a frightful rolling about. And only a few of their skippers care to tackle the navigational challenges of fog and tide. The masted vessels all pass outside Great Wass Island and lie at the Mudhole, the Cowyard, or Roque Island.

At the very end of the road stood the laundromat, steamy and soapy, frequented by the busy housewives of Jonesport. Yet they had time to help us with the idiosyncracies of the machines and to call us "deah." In Jonesport it used to be "chum." It is reported that a coaster, lost in the fog and hearing a dory approaching, hailed.

"Where am I?"

"What's that, chum?"

"Never mind. I'm in Jonesport."

Laden with clean clothes, we paraded back the length of the street, stopping for supplies at the supermarket. Wheaties, Bounty towels, Del Monte peaches, Royal gelatine, it was the same as any other market, but the checkout lady took our check.

"You look honest, deah."

We passed up lunch at Ginny's restaurant, for we were short of money, and staggered aboard, starved to death, to a sumptuous meal punctuated by the staccato rhythms of the hoisting engine on the wharf.

Mary and I rowed up the shore a way to get ice, passing a solitary man in a small sloop who was waiting serenely for tide and weather to turn. He called to mind another singlehander in Cape Split.

With three boys for crew and in company with another sloop carrying a skipper and two boys, we were laying over a day there in the fog. A large supper of hamburger was in preparation for all hands. Out of the fog ghosted an ancient gaff-rigged racing sloop. Her solitary skipper hailed us in a strong Southern accent, asking for a restaurant. There was none. We invited him aboard for supper, an invitation accepted with startling alacrity.

"I'm hungry as a b'ar 'cause I hates to cook. Been living on beer and bananas." He had been out at the Cowyard on the southern end of Head Harbor Island where there is no restaurant, store, or anything else but a summer cottage, owned, he declared, by one Horace de Forest. Horace was away, leaving his wife and daughter in residence. When this hairy gorilla came prowling about seeking innocently to buy a can of beans — anything but beer and bananas — they naturally barred the door and made no answer. So Beer-and-Bananas retired aboard his sloop to write poems, several of which we set to music at once and sang with vigor.

> Oh Horace de Forest has vittles to spare.
> Vittles delicious are Horace's fare;
> But I on my boat
> Have the fare of a goat,
> For Horace de Forest his vittles won't share.

There are more super-normal people on the water than on the land!

Back aboard we found the sun shining through the fog and an occasional scale-up showing the bridge and a loom of Beals Island across the Reach. Renewed calculations showed that we could not get under the bridge. Jonesport had lost its charm for us so we took the last of the flood tide and ran back to Roque through the choking-thick fog. As Captain Ed said of fog runs long ago, "It's all right if you make all right." With a good helmsman and a good lookout, the navigator can devote full attention to time, course, distance and depth, sure that his courses are being followed and that he will be informed of the sudden appearance of beacon, ledge, or pot buoy. But if time runs out and the mark is not sighted — if one does not "make" all right — one can be just as badly lost and just as catastrophically wrecked in Mooseabec Reach as in deep water offshore.

We "made all right" except for one minor confusion, and that is about the best one can expect. Navigation as taught in schools may be an exact science. Its triangles, its neat arithmetic, its bearings all in precise degrees work out beautifully in the classroom. However, "The chart is not the sea," as the poet said. If we are fortunate enough to be in a locality listed in the current tables, we must correct the tabulated figure for the effects of the wind, the phase of the moon and the state of the sea. Mostly we just look at a passing pot buoy, guess at a good knot of tide, and call it half a knot because we always overestimate. We have an instrument to measure out speed to the nearest tenth of a knot but it is as often referred to as "the little liar" as by its proper name. Under power, if the engine sounds busy and happy, we call it five knots, one mile in twelve minutes. Under sail, we look at the bubbles going by and take a hot guess. No one can steer a small boat closer than a quarter point — two degrees — either side of the course and few helmsmen are attentive and skillful enough to do that. I assume the depth indicator is about right, but that is only because I don't know enough about it to understand its errors. So, precise as the science may be, on the chart table of a small boat we approach every calculation with trepidation and hope the errors will cancel each other out. We sail the course with profound suspicion and are relieved when so frequently we "make."

The wisest thing a navigator can do is to keep quiet. There is little to be gained by telling the world of his uncertainty and thus spreading apprehension. Let him do the best he can and take credit for being a miracle man when, by a combination of luck and compensating errors, he succeeds.

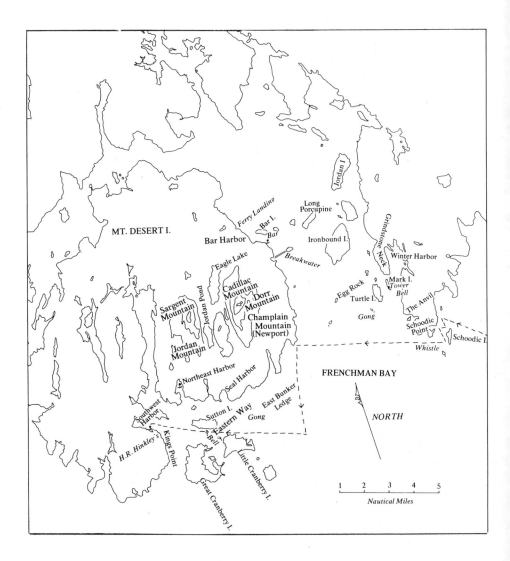

MT. DESERT I.

Ferry Landing

Bar Harbor

Eagle Lake

Cadillac
Mountain

Sargent
Mountain

Jordan Pond

Dorr
Mountain

Champlain
Mountain
(Newport)

Jordan
Mountain

Bar I.
Bar

Breakwater

Long
Porcupine

Ironbound I.

Jordan I.

Grindstone Neck

Winter Harbor

Mark I.
Tower
Bell

Egg Rock

Turtle I.

Gong

The Anvil

Schoodic
Point

Schoodic I

Whistle

Northeast Harbor

Seal Harbor

Southwest
Harbor

Sutton I.

Eastern Way

Gong

East Bunker
Ledge

FRENCHMAN BAY

NORTH

H.R. Hinkley's

Kings Point

Bell

Little Cranberry I.

Great Cranberry I.

1   2   3   4   5

Nautical Miles

26 Three Vignettes

The start in a light northerly, the fog thinning. Bright blue overhead, solid white vapor all around. The disc of the sun visible occasionally through thinner spots. Fair wind but very light — mainsail broad off but the sheet sagging and tripping the surface. The sea silky — not a ripple, an easy roll swashing on the invisible shore to port. Sounds of a Maine morning: crows, young crows, picking at mussels bared by the ebbing tide and talking about it, not in loud "caws" but in hoarse conversational tones. A gull screaming his unrestrained enthusiasm for food; another gull overhead in swift, silent flight headed off to port to investigate. The distant, clear note of the bell off Mark Island and the harsh clank as the clapper swings back against the restraining bar. Ahead to starboard the high, sweet note of the Canadian white-throat in the woods of Mark Island.

Then the engine again lest the tide turn against us before we make Black Head. When the wind comes southerly, we shut it off.

'Tit Manan: First a distant bellow on the starboard bow, coming down on the gentle southwesterly air, *Eastward* picking her way close-hauled through the little tide chop. A flash, high off the horizon,

143

through the thinning fog: The light always shows when the horn is going — automatically. Then the outline of the lantern and suddenly the tall, brown, stone tower, delicate in the mist and dazzle of sun and fog. Below the tower, seeming to be unaware of it, the tiny dwelling, the low engine house, the boathouse on the sheltered side, its roof and eave line pitched to conform to the pitch of the boat skids. The island is low, a sprinkle of grass, a low line of white ledge, brown weed, white surf. A warm, peaceful summer scene today, yet with that disciplined aloof tower, its regular flash and regular fog blast, full of menace. Imagine it looming through snow, not fog, with gray seas driven before a winter southeaster cresting on the shoals, shouldering each other in the tide, crashing to run roaring white over the low island, battering the dwelling; but the tower stands, unmoved, not deigning to notice. On the distant coast, miles to the north in the snug harbors at Cape Split, Corea, and Prospect Harbor, where lights flicker in the early winter dusk, family men look out.

In a dying breeze, ghosting up the Eastern Way. Astern lies Frenchman Bay, Schoodic Point, so far ahead of us at noon, so clear, so close aboard in mid-afternoon, now fading in the dusk. Behind Schoodic is 'Tit Manan, the fog and the cold, scouring Fundy tides, the dark woods of Roque, the barren hump of Libby Island, the cliffs of Grand Manan. To port the nearby lights of Cranberry Island, to starboard the rounded hills of Mt. Desert — like a procession of docile elephants — purple against the sunset. At the base of the hills the lights of Northeast Harbor and of cars on Peabody Drive heading for the movies or a restaurant or the campground or the bright lights of Bar Harbor — or just driving. A powerboat crosses ahead towing three small, tall sloops, bound home from the afternoon races. They are being towed much too fast, each one squatting down aft and pulling back on the towline with feet braced, yanked along anyway like recalcitrant little boys behind an impatient mother. A big launch comes by with a great sign, ISLESBORO FERRY, on the top of the house, three children in the bow, a man in shorts and a white sweater leaning against the rail around the stern. The wash advances at us, curling across the still water, slaps our side, rolls ʳhe last of the wind out of the mainsail and topsail and leaves us flat becalmed.

I start the engine. We are back on the edge of suburbia.

Crossing Frenchman Bay bound west. The Eastern Way is under the lee bow. (Prenatt)

27 Black Back and Shag

We lay on a mooring that night in Southwest Harbor after a fine dinner constructed by Harold out of macaroni, cheese, pepperoni and more subtle ingredients. As the regular cook, I was delighted to have someone else exercise his genius, for mine has worn a bit thin over the years. I got into the cooking business when I started cruising with boys. Cap Williams and I cruised in company — he in the 24-foot *Helen G* and I in the 28-foot *Dorothy*. We took five boys with the intention of showing them how to have a good time on the water in a safe and civilized manner. Part of the program was to be instruction in cooking. However, after a very brief trial period of rotating the *cordon bleu*, in self-defense I took over the job. Ample instruction and experience in dishwashing may have compensated.

Over the years supply lists, menus and procedures have become standardized. For the quick meal, pressure-cooked potatoes fried with salt pork, onions, and a can of corned beef will do the job. When the sun gets low, the afternoon southerly is cold, and the anchorage is still a long way to windward, a pilot cracker, peanut butter and a chocolate ration is immediately issued. Then I fire up the Shipmate stove and put in the oven a canned ham, pan of chicken, or whatever I can find. As we get closer, the pressure-cooker of potatoes with an onion or two goes on top of the stove. If opportunity serves, a pan of instant cornbread mix can go on the lower

The yachting fleet at anchor off Hinckley's yard, Manset,
Maine. (Prenatt)

shelf of the oven. No further attention is necessary.

When the anchor is on the bottom, the sails furled and the first stars show, the cabin is warm and dry and dinner is ready at once. We can tell that we have been sailing, for the cornbread will be deep on one side and shoal on the other according to which tack we were on.

After a month afloat, though, the crew gets used to the nature of the menu — boiled potatoes, hamburg, canned ham, fried fish — so Harold's dinner was a real celebration.

After dinner we went ashore to visit a lady, now a mathematics professor at a distinguished college and author of a book, to me inscrutable, on the pleasures of higher mathematics. I knew her first, however, as a tough, blocky, straight-haired fourteen-year-old at a coed sailing camp on the Sheepscot River. She proved to be the most able and interested of my charges. On one occasion she saved the girls' cruise from probable disaster.

We cruised in three boats: *Dorothy*, of which I was skipper, *Helen G*, of which Cap Williams was skipper, and *Sequoia*, a power-boat with a huge cockpit, roof, and detachable curtains, commanded by Commodore Allen, director of the camp. We cruised in company, the three skippers sleeping aboard *Helen G*.

On a hot, windy, southwest day we beat up to Portland and anchored the convoy on the east side of the harbor opposite the old Portland Yacht Club. Cap Williams and the Commodore went ashore in the Commodore's skiff. Feeling very rocky from some questionable hash consumed the night before, I lay down on a bunk aboard *Dorothy*. About five of the girls, including our future math professor, set out across the choppy waters of Portland Harbor in a square-sided, peak-nosed skiff, which in still water might have had three inches of freeboard. One of the girls was on crutches with a cast on her broken ankle.

Predictably, the chop began to slop over the side. Jill at the oars urged her crew to bail, but shoes and hats proved inadequate. The skiff swamped and turned over. At once Jill got the cripple on the top of the skiff, swam around collecting crutches and oars, and got the others to hang on to the sides of the boat. She then swam over to a near-by steam yacht and hailed a uniformed sailor lounging on the stern. His eyes popped and he disappeared. Presently an officer with an elaborate cap appeared, stared, and he too disappeared. Then a genuine white-flannelled, blue-blazered Owner appeared. Whistles blew. A boat was lowered, the girls were rescued and brought aboard where they dripped on the immaculate teak. The owner made them welcome, and took them ashore to the Portland Yacht Club, towing the skiff. The first I knew of it was when Jill's head appeared in the hatch, her hair plastered down so she looked like an angry seal. "Those fool girls dumped the skiff."

Now we sat in her comfortable living room thirty-five years later and did not feel much changed.

During the night we were dimly aware of distant lightning and a rumble of thunder. The morning dawned crystalline — a summer northerly. This is what we wait all winter for. As we stood down the Western Way, the sun shone warm and the air smelled of Katahdin and the north woods, the hills behind us stood sharply green and gray against the bright northern sky. The shores of Cranberry Island and Kings Point were brilliant white backed with vivid green. The breakers on South Bunker Ledge flashed. With that exalted feeling expressed so clearly in *Oklahoma* — "Everything's going my way" — we rounded Long Ledge, passed the picture-postcard light on Bass Harbor Bar and stood across Blue Hill Bay. At York Narrows we entered one of the loveliest parts of Maine. Here are innumerable little islands, some merely ledges, others a mile long, ringed with smooth white granite and crowned with spruce. Narrow sandy beaches lie between the boulders on the shore and open places among the woods are crowded with juniper, sweet fern, vetch and bayberry. Lobster trap buoys warn of shoal water and government buoys mark the main channels through Deer Island Thorofare and Merchants Row. On such a day as this, what more can Heaven offer?

In the middle of Jericho Bay as it fell calm, we met a great black-backed gull with an adolescent sense of humor. Flying slowly just above the surface of the water, he approached us and circled the boat. He held a fish in his beak. Just behind him, in frantic pursuit, came a shag, probably the rightful owner of the fish. Black Back flew with slow, powerful strokes, chuckling low through the fish. Shag gained altitude, closed in. Black Back circled closer to us, preventing Shag from turning inside him. Shag closed a little more. Black Back accelerated, gained altitude, swung close ahead of our bowsprit, and dropped Shag astern. Silently, doggedly, angrily, Shag sprinted to hold his position, but dropped back. Black Back chuckled and cut off Shag by swooping insolently close to our boom on a clean glide. Three loons laughed. There was no denouement, for after another circle Black Back went off to the northwest, still carrying the fish, still chuckling, with Shag still in stubborn pursuit and with the loons still much amused.

Then the wind struck in gently from the south and we worked our way through the islands north of Isle au Haut. We contemplated stopping at McGlathery, but it was early afternoon, the breeze still held, and we wanted to get to Friendship the next day. Through the glasses we could see the mound of rotting boards and shingles where the Mayor's house had stood, and we passed by.

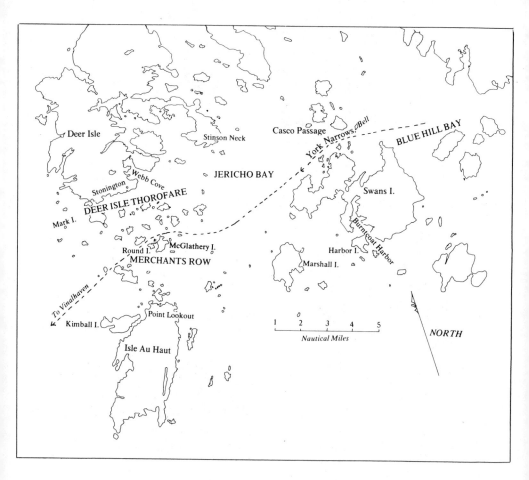

28 The Mayor of McGlathery Island

During the winter of 1937-38, after our summer at the sailing camp, Cap Williams and I organized Apprentice Cruises, our scheme described in a previous chapter for teaching boys the pleasures of civilized cruising. We even designed a house flag with a D for Duncan and a W for Williams. The boys later concluded it stood for Dead to Windward.

Between — or instead of — college examination reviews, we studied charts, looking for uninhabited out-of-the-way anchorages where we could swim, go clamming, fish, pick berries, and roam ashore. The islands between Isle au Haut and Stonington seemed promising and the harbor between McGlathery and Round Island looked ideal.

In July, after a southeaster spent at anchor off Point Lookout on Isle au Haut, we ran up to Webbs Cove and walked to Stonington for supplies. Because we felt the boys needed exercise and because we heard that a yacht had burned in the Thorofare and gone ashore, we marched our squad down to survey the wreck. There wasn't much to see. It was low tide and the boys picked over the charred wreckage in search of souvenirs. Someone found a fork.

On a small wharf left dry by the tide sat two fishermen. One I don't remember. The other was a little man, no more than five feet tall, thin, wiry, alert. I made some sententious remark about having a fire extinguisher handy. The little man burst out.

Naamon Hutchinson, Mayor of McGlathery, aboard the
City Hall about 1938.

"Them fire distinguishers, they ain't worth a peehole in the snow."
He continued as if he had been dammed up for a week. "I was going
down to Isle au Haut with a load of bait. She *back*fired and *ig*-nited,
down under the bait. I seen my fire distinguisher and I put it to her;
flames blazed up higher 'n ever. I got out on the bow and says, 'It's
a hell of a ways to swim ashore, Naamon, when you can't swim!'
Then I see my draw bucket and I says, '*Now*, by Jesus Christ, I got
you,' and I poked her out."

We stood astonished, awed by the quick, vivid picture and the
blaze of emotion about fire extinguishers. Humbly we inquired
about McGlathery. We might as well have asked Moses about the
Promised Land! The dam broke again. The anchorage was good,
the island uninhabited, the flats alive with clams, the water with
flounder and the woods with berries. He seemed to feel an instant
sympathy with us and our boys, told us of a weir that was fishing on
the bar where we might catch mackerel and of a spring of good water
he had dug out under a sand bank. Furthermore, he made the place
his headquarters, living there aboard his boat to be near the lobstering. He urged us to visit him. We left, feeling we would never know

peace again until our fleet swung to its anchors in McGlathery's harbor.

The next day, a cool, quiet, cloudy day with the fog curling off the tops of the islands, we fanned in about four o'clock, dropped anchor near a battered lobsterboat with a bit of stovepipe sticking up through her cuddy, and went ashore to explore. It was just as Naamon had described it. Sheep ran on the island and made paths through the spruce thickets, leaving bits of wool on the bushes. We found the spring. We found on a knoll overlooking the harbor a gravestone with the name of Peter Eaton. We walked around the shore toward the weir over a smooth gravel beach and a white granite ledge. We saw no sign of human inhabitants.

Following a sheep path — easy if you are no taller than a sheep — we came out on a little sandy beach. A small lobsterboat lay with her bows just aground, her stern afloat. On the beach four people sat around the smoldering ashes of a fire with the last of a gallon jug of red rum punch. Naamon waved the jug in greeting and urged us to join the party. The owner of the boat was his cousin Pearl. The two ladies I never got straight. We joined the party.

Pearl declared with a seriousness and a certainty doubtless imbibed from the jug that he could put his ankle behind his neck. General doubt was expressed. Pearl seized his foot, strained mightily, and rolled over in the sand. One of our boys, more limber at fourteen than the much older Pearl, easily performed the feat. Pearl, feeling the tide of public approval setting against him, tried again, rolled over again, but did not give up trying. And then he did it! He actually got his right ankle behind his neck. The tide of approval turned at once and everyone cheered. Pearl, half choked by the constriction of his neck and straining every stretched ligament, grinned in triumph.

But he couldn't get his leg down again. He heaved and struggled helplessly and the fickle tide of public approval turned again. At last we had to help him and then administer a dose of medicine out of the jug to soothe his wrenched joints and wounded morale.

Just as we drifted back to normal, we saw that Pearl's lobster-boat was drifting back to Stonington. It was still close to shore but we had no skiff. Pearl pleaded for one of us to swim off and get it. Cap Williams stripped to his shorts, plunged in, and climbed aboard to renewed cheers from shore.

"Start her up," yelled Pearl.

Cap Williams had not the least idea of how to start her up. He had never owned a boat with an engine. He stood shivering in his wet shorts and drifted off. However, he found an oar in the cockpit and assuming the air of a gondolier, though clad somewhat less elaborately, paddled shoreward. More cheers.

In appreciation, Pearl caught up a can of beer, a survivor of the lobster feed just finished, and tossed it to him. Hugh dropped the oar to catch the can, but another was already in the air. He dropped the first to catch the second, and dexterously kept ahead of the hail of beer as Pearl grabbed the bow and made it fast to a tree.

Then we all had a beer and talked about the island. Naamon declared he was the only inhabitant. We at once constituted ourselves a body politic and by acclamation elected him Mayor and declared his boat the City Hall.

We came back to McGlathery again and again, together and separately, bringing crews of boys, then our wives, and then our own children. Our own boys, cruising with other groups, formed the habit of dropping in. The Mayor was almost always there, first in the City Hall, later in a tent, and then in a camp on Round Island with a lady we knew as Hattie. Often there would be other guests, too. I came ashore one Fourth of July and was urged at ten a.m. to have a drink.

"What are you drinking?" I asked.

"Gin."

"I don't care much for gin in the morning."

"Oh hell, none of us like it but it's all we got."

That day I saw Uncle Arch, a long, lean lobsterman who hauled traps by hand and who could chin himself on a spruce tree with one hand, the other held behind him. The boys ran races around the island, we murdered a shag with a shotgun and "roasted" it for dinner, and celebrated that anniversary of American Independence with éclat.

Little by little through the years we learned that Naamon had lived around Penobscot Bay all his life, had been lobstering in dories, peapods and sloops, fishing offshore in schooners, coasting in the granite trade, yachting as paid hand on the great pre-World War I schooner yachts and on steam yachts. He told us of a fast passage in the old *Annie & Reuben*, a stone schooner with a huge foresail, on which he ate breakfast before sunrise under Charlestown Bridge, Boston, and dinner after sunset under Green Head, Stonington, running before a smoky sou'wester all the way. He told of the wreck of a three-masted coaster in Nantucket Sound one winter. As she lay at anchor on the shoals, her sails blown out, the skipper set a bottle of rum on the cabin table and told the hands to help themselves. The cook, unemployed on deck, did so more liberally than the rest. The anchor chain parted and they abandoned the vessel in the yawl boat when, through the snow, they got a glimmer of the Cross Rip Lightship.

"I'm going to die. I'm going to die," complained the cook.

"Well die and be damned to you," the Mayor had said. Then he added hastily to us, "I never would have said it if I'd have known he was going to do it."

They made the lightship and left the yawl boat tied astern with the cook's body in it. During the night the thwart around which the painter was tied pulled out and they never saw cook or boat again.

The Mayor took us lobstering with him and showed us how to dig clams — "For Chrissake, Roger, get your arse downhill." He remembered my name from a limerick about Roger the Lodger but called Cap Williams "the other feller." He was always glad to see us come and sorry to see us go. He was hospitable, enthusiastic, and always interesting. He had a nephew called June, short for Junior, who lived with him several summers and taught our boys a lot they never learned in school. We never had a dull day at McGlathery.

Once we stood together on the shore of Round Island in the thick fog with the sun shining down through it from a milky-blue sky. I wanted to get to the westward and looked up hopefully.

"It's clear overhead, Naamon."

"I know, Roger, but the hell of it is we ain't bound that way."

At last in the 1950's the Mayor died. The camp fell down. The piles of buoys and the lobster traps disappeared from the shore. The weir ceased to be profitable and fell apart. The spring silted up. Now cruise schooners anchor off the beach where we elected the Mayor of McGlathery Island and yachts begin to crowd the harbor. Brush has grown up around Peter Eaton's grave, but I can still find the stone.

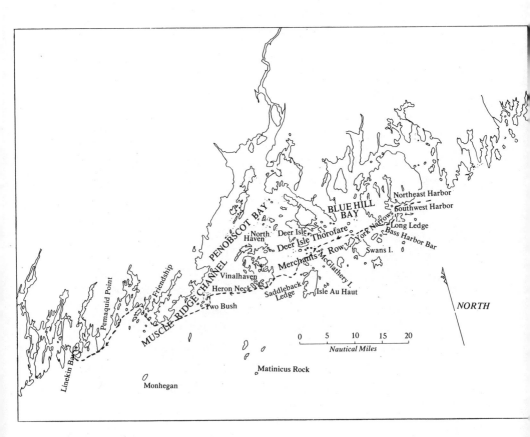

29 Emergencies

So we sailed by McGlathery this time, south to Saddleback Ledge where the light keepers used to bring us ashore on a bosun's chair hung from a derrick boom, and beat into Vinalhaven against the tide in the sunset. In the morning, Bob and Mary went ashore to visit a large stone eagle standing on the main street. Years before, when Vinalhaven had been a great granite town and the harbor was crowded with barges and schooners carrying paving blocks and building stone to Boston, New York, and Philadelphia, skilled stonecutters worked in the quarries. From Vinalhaven came the stone for the Pennsylvania Station in New York. The stone eagles which used to stand superciliously above New York traffic were cut in Vinalhaven, and when their usefulness in New York was over, one was brought home as a memorial to the granite industry. This huge stone fowl now stands with his back to the harbor, his wings half spread, and an expression of utter scorn on his face. *Sic transit . . . .*

As frequently happens with the passage of a summer cold front, the wind was northerly at first and carried us out past Folly Ledge and Heron Neck. Two cruise schooners lay becalmed outside, having left just ahead of us. In the 1920's, looking out from New Harbor, it was no rare sight to see two-masted, three-masted, and even four-masted coasters working alongshore between Allen Island and Monhegan. The old *William Keene* used to visit New Harbor every summer with salt and carry away barrels of fish. Later the *Lillian* took up the job. In the early thirties we sailed up Boothbay Harbor at dusk one evening to see three great four-masters anchored there. However, they were to be laid up in the mud of Mill Cove where their bones still lie. In August, 1938, we boarded the three-master *Thomas H. Lawrence*, loaded with pilings for the World's Fair in New York, and in 1940 saw the four-master *Theoline* loaded with coal alongside a Stonington wharf. Some of it was transferred into the smaller two-masters *Enterprise* and *Endeavor*, to be distributed to island communities. But this was about the last commercial schooner trade on the coast.

Captain Frank Swift, in 1935, taking a hint from the "dude ranches" of the West, fitted up the little schooner *Clinton* with bunks in her hold for passengers and began sailing one-week parties out of Camden. We saw her in 1938. In 1941 we saw the *Philosopher* alongside a wharf in Bucks Harbor, her hold half full of hay and her decks crowded with exuberant youngsters in green shorts from Robin Hood Camp. Fred Littlefield, director of the camp, also clad in green shorts and equally exuberant, told me that if I wanted to expand Apprentice Cruises, I could run such an operation some day! So far, I have avoided that fate.

Captain Swift's fleet rapidly expanded until it included, among others, *Enterprise, Endeavor, Lois M. Candage, Annie F. Kimball, Mattie, Mercantile, Stephen Taber, Eva S. Cullison,* and *Alice T. Wentworth*. *Victory Chimes*, the only three-master, still sails parties under Captain Boyd Guild. Then the fleet began to shrink as the old hulls rotted out. However, a few enterprising skippers have built new schooners for the trade. Among these are *Mary Day, Harvey Gamage, Bill of Rights,* and *Shenandoah*, the last a lovely vessel with square topsails on her foremast. *Mattie, Mercantile,* and *Stephen Taber* still sail and a number of yachts have been converted for the trade. A Gloucester fishing schooner, *Adventure*, has joined the fleet. The Arctic exploration vessel, *Bowdoin*, while not carrying passengers commercially, is still seen under sail. Although their decks are crowded with gaily-dressed, or undressed, vacationers and the cook serves salads instead of "salt horse," it is good to see gaff-headed schooners on Penobscot Bay and occasionally to meet someone who knows how to set a topsail.

The wind at length came in southerly and the schooners stood off toward Matinicus while we headed westward across Penobscot Bay on the last of the ebb tide. It soon turned against us and we settled down to a long, long beat around Two Bush in a moderate air.

Two Bush is a bare little island with a lighthouse and dwelling on it so designed that to the quick and casual glance it looks like the superstructure of a naval vessel. It lies at the southern extremity of the islands of the Muscle Ridges and is guarded by a long, ugly reef extending to the eastward. With the tide flooding east by the island and north up the bay, progress against the southwest breeze is slow. The best chance is to stand close in under the islands and get the stronger breeze coming off them. This we did, finding smoother

Former coasting schooners sailing parties south of Vinalhaven. (Prenatt)

water, too, but as we stood off to the point from which at last we could fetch by the reef and the island, we heard a heavy *clunk* — something, somewhere, had parted under heavy strain.

It was no shroud, for they were new. But the bowsprit was standing almost on end and looking at us! We got the jib down in a hurry and found that the shackle holding the bobstay to the heavy eye bolted through the stem at the waterline had rusted through.

Hanging over the bow with Bob holding my ankles, I got a line and a double block fast to the eye on the stem. We set up the other end of the tackle to the end of the bowsprit and hove taut, but the tackle twisted up so we could not get it very tight, and when we set the jib, the dacron line stretched so much that our jury rig did little good. However, after we got into smooth water we found that we could set the jib if Bob stood on the end of the bowsprit and Harold eased the jib sheet in the puffs.

Because we make all the gear on our sloop heavy enough for a coasting schooner, we seldom part anything, but every skipper sooner or later must improvise a jury rig or at least react intelligently to a sudden failure of something he trusts. Twice we have lost topmasts — both times picturesquely.

The first time, we were bound up the Saint John River with a fair southerly breeze. Astern of us came a fleet of fine, large yachts bulging with spinnakers but not catching us very fast. As it breezed up, we hung on to the topsail, hoping to keep ahead of the fleet as long as possible. Caution urged setting up a backstay from the top of the topmast to the quarter bitts. The only problem was that if we gybed over, the boom and gaff would hit the backstay and put an intolerable strain on the topmast. So when I turned the wheel over to Mary, I urged her to have a knife ready to cut the backstay pennant if a gybe started. But no gybe came and all was well, the modern fleet gaining but slowly on the last century.

As we approached a turn in the river, it appeared that we would have to gybe. Not so, thought I. We will tack and avoid sudden and violent strain on the gear. I let go the jib sheet, rolled the wheel down and rounded in the mainsheet. As she came slatting through the eye of the wind, I dropped the mainsheet, grabbed the new lee jib sheet and paid off on the other tack. But Mary noticed the burgee in the water alongside! I looked up and gasped — astounded. Instead of the usual orderly and dignified topmast rigging, I saw a jagged stump standing three feet above the lower masthead and the rest of the topmast, topsail and gear hanging over the spreaders in disarray. The strap holding the halyard for the burgee had dropped off the masthead as it hung upside down.

Being in shoal water, we simply dropped headsails, thankful for downhauls, anchored, and started to clear up the mess. As we were getting the wreckage on deck, the first of the fleet rushed by, a lovely red yawl manned by the owner, his wife and a mutual friend. The lady had her hands full steering and the two gentlemen were forward engaged in gybing a gigantic spinnaker. As they swished by, the owner called, "Can we help you?"

I appreciated the offer, but we were comfortably anchored and he seemed in imminent danger of being swung over the side on one end of a mad spinnaker pole. I declined the offer.

The other time we lost a topmast was equally exciting, for we were in a race in which we did not belong and, in the face of a big, black squall, were hanging on to our full rig just as long as we could, of course with backstay taut. As the squall rushed at us, we luffed to douse topsail and jib. With the sails half down, the wind shifted suddenly, from southwest to northwest, slapped the mainsail against the backstay, and down came the topmast again. With the spar held forward by the jib topsail stay and sideways by the topmast shrouds, the sudden strain from aft must have been converted into thrust downward and that fine Sitka spruce topmast must have bent like Robin Hood's bow before it broke off short.

Another time, with a fine breeze blowing, we parted the three-eighth-inch dacron jackstay which holds the topsail against the topmast. We took in the topsail, of course, and continued the afternoon's sail, most of our passengers pretty much unaware of what had happened. However, as the afternoon wore on, the breeze sagged and I began to wish we had a topsail set. To while away the time, I spliced up a new jackstay; but to rig it, I would have to go aloft. One of our passengers, I noticed, was a powerful man with upper arms as big as my leg. He was a shipfitter at the Bath Iron Works and was building a sloop himself. We got to wishing together that we could set the topsail, so finally I asked him if he would mind hoisting me aloft on the jib topsail halyard. I never had such a fast ride up a mast in my life. I went up like a rocket. Then, swinging gently in a bosun's chair halfway up the topmast, I could look down on the gaff, the ensign at the peak, the sweep of mainsail, now fore-shortened, to the deck and the tops of people's heads. I could sense how a gull felt about people on boats. The motion was easy. We were heeled enough so I was out over the water. Very restful, I thought. Very pleasant. But there are still marks on the fir topmast where I was clutching it.

30 Friendship Sloops and the Friendship Sloop Society

The Friendship Sloop Society was conceived in a moment of triumph in September 1960. The Boston Power Squadron, as a fitting way to end the season on a cheerful note, held a "Bang and Go Back" race for auxiliaries. A fleet comprising everything from tightly-tuned ocean racers to slack-stayed backyard boats started together and reached out to sea. After an hour or so, another gun was fired. Everyone tacked and headed for home. The first one in was to be the winner.

Bernard MacKenzie was the proud owner of the Friendship sloop *Voyager* built down east in the early years of the century as a lobster-boat. When she had been converted to a yacht, her mainsail had been radically shortened so it was chronically double-reefed. Consequently she had no great reputation for speed. When the turn-around gun boomed, *Voyager* tacked and found that the last was first.

The wind breezed up very fresh and hauled aft a little. *Voyager* had it right on the quarter where she liked it and with her reduced mainsail was properly dressed for the occasion. Ballooning spinnakers threatened from astern. Bernie MacKenzie writes: "We had no spinnaker aboard *Voyager*: only a huge gaff mainsail like those used to get fish to market long ago. Could we hold out with eight miles to go? We kept an eye on a blue-hulled splinter astern which was

slowly closing the gap. That was *Contessa*. Then a touch of luck.
The wind increased. We drove with a comber under our bow and a
quarter-beam [sic] wave under our stern, signaling that this was hull
speed and she would go no faster. We had come on a reach to follow
the course between two islands when *BANG!* our jib split from peak
to clew!

"It took all three of the crew to get this down and another set,
while our race observer steered, eating humble pie for saying earlier
that he thought Friendships were logy!

"Due to the delay with the jib, one of the big fellows was right on
top of us, but going through the gut his parachute pulled him over,
right down to the water. He would come up with tons of water pour-
ing out of his chute, only to have it immersed again.

"Running free in Quincy Bay we were actually gaining on the
fleet and we opened up a half mile lead not having to worry about
spinnakers. The crew was joyous as we approached the lonely committee boat, having clocked seven knots between the last two buoys.

"The flash of the cannon cut through the stillness of the autumn
afternoon . . . ."

Bernie, his friend Earl Banner of the *Boston Globe*, and a number
of Friendship residents including Postmaster Carlton Simmons, who
had built a Friendship sloop; the Lash brothers, who ran a boatshop
in Hatchet Cove; Al and Betty Roberts, who bought lobsters in
Friendship; Herald Jones, Sid Prior, and a number of other local
people touched off the Friendship Sloop Society.

Over the last thirteen years the Society has solved some knotty
problems, but it has not yet succeeded in defining a Friendship sloop
with any degree of precision. A Friendship sloop is a little like a
whale or a bald eagle. It is hard to describe one so a stranger will
understand it, but once he has seen one, he will never need to have
it defined. A clipper bow, a quick perky sheer, a low, broad gaff-
headed mainsail of inordinate acreage, one or two headsails, hard
bilges aft, a hollow bow, and a long, straight keel are characteristic
of most Friendships; but it is the buoyant, businesslike way she sits
on the water, the grace that comes not from chrome and varnish but

from form matched to function, that really defines her. Once you have seen one afloat, you will never have to ask again; and until that time, I can't help you much.

The Friendship sloop evolved in the last twenty years of the last century in response to the demand for a fast, able fishing boat for lobstering and 'longshore fishing. One side of the family was the little Muscongus Bay sloop, a centerboarder, usually plumb-bowed and clinker built, seldom over twenty-six feet long. The other side was the new Gloucester fishing schooner *Fredonia*, designed by Edward Burgess, fast, able, and breathlessly handsome. *Fredonia's* lines were adapted to the Gloucester sloop-boats and then developed by Muscongus Bay builders into what became famous as the Friendship sloop.

Wilbur Morse, who probably built more sloops of this type than anyone else, built his first boat in 1875 and by 1900 had a busy shop in Friendship turning out sloops for Maine fishermen at a rapid rate. However, they were not, like Ford cars, all the same. If Sam wanted one like George's, only a mite finer under the quarter, the molds would be fined down a little here or shimmed out a little there. Wilbur Morse's yard built little boats from twenty to twenty-four feet long for lobstering in among the ledges and big ones up to twice that size for offshore fishing and lobstering and for carrying fish and lobsters "up" to Portland and Boston and running back "downeast" with freight. To add to the variety, Wilbur Morse was by no means the only man building sloops. Several other Morses turned out one or two or three boats a year and the Carters, McClains, Priors, and Winchenbachs, among others, built fine, able sloops. Their sons and grandsons added their own variations. So a Friendship sloop is at once indefinable and unmistakable.

While Friendship sloops were being built as fishing boats, they developed high, sharp bows with a wide flare to knife through a chop and still keep their crews reasonably dry. They were built with a generous beam, about one third of the overall length, so they would be stiff and provide a stable platform from which to haul handlines and lobster traps. The mast was stepped far forward so that the boat could be sailed up a line of traps with mainsail alone. The Friendship sloop was heavily sparred and carried a press of sail. Her main boom was traditionally equal to the waterline length and is reminiscent of the booms on Gloucester schooners. In Maine, the summer days are often very gentle and it takes a big mainsail to move a heavy boat. Some sloops even carried gaff topsails and jib topsails in the summer. Take them any way they came, though, they would take you out and bring you back.

By July, 1961, the Society was well enough organized to hold a regatta in which eleven sloops raced. We had heard of the affair where we were party-boating out of Newagen, near Boothbay Harbor. We were not racing people but it looked like fun so we went up to Friendship through a dungeon of fog to "try her out."

We rather suspected we might have a chance at the hardware: A week before the races Mr. Winthrop Bancroft had chartered *Eastward* to see if he would like to have a Friendship sloop built for himself. He inspected every detail of *Eastward*, asked many intelligent questions and sailed the boat for a while. He told us that he had just been in Friendship where they were gearing up for the regatta and had seen *Mary Anne*, a new sloop just finished by the Lash Brothers' yard. She was said to be very fast — the boat to beat. He did not really believe we could take her. Then he told us of a new Sparkman & Stevens cutter he had seen launched the day before at Paul Luke's yard in Linekin Bay. He was sure she was the fastest yacht that ever spread a mainsail and, like all of Paul Luke's boats, elegantly finished. So we sailed over that way to inspect her.

As we approached, she left the float on her trial sail. Of course we knew we couldn't keep up with her so we passed to leeward, tacked under her stern, and followed just to windward of her wake. *Eastward* got the bit in her teeth edged a bit to windward, and sailed right by that cutter and went on her dignified way home. Mr. Bancroft couldn't believe it. We were delighted. Of course the new boat had never stretched her sails or rigging, she had not been tuned up at all, and her new owner had not learned how to make her do her best. Nevertheless, we headed for Friendship with high hopes and Mr.

Bancroft headed for South Bristol where he commissioned Murray Peterson to design him another *Eastward*.

Mary Anne was fast and her skipper got her off to a good start, but *Eastward* at last overhauled her and beat her by twenty minutes at the finish. The gun was a genuine six-pounder from the War of 1812. The gunner fired a flaming wad of oakum into our cockpit to signal the victory. Bernie MacKenzie won the Governor's Cup for the first old-timer to finish and we took home the Lash Brothers trophy for the fastest replica.

Since then the Society and the regatta has steadily grown.

On Tuesday night, July 24, 1973, Friendship harbor was already beginning to fill up with sloops anchored along both shores. There were old sloops, built, rebuilt, and some of them rebuilt again from

Eastward leads the fleet across the finish line in an early Friendship regatta.

stem to gudgeon so they were rather like George Washington's axe. We had to replace the handle and we had to get a new head, but we still own George Washington's axe. There were some quite new wooden boats too, several built by Lash Brothers in Hatchet Cove from a scaled-down model made by Wilbur Morse and now in the hands of Winfield Lash. Yet even these, all built more or less to the same plan, vary a good deal. And we saw several fiberglass Friendship sloops. It seems heretical, an inherent contradiction, to suggest that such a traditional old vessel could be made of a modern material. However, Jarvis Newman in Southwest Harbor used a replica of Abdon Carter's *Pemaquid* for a plug and came out with a lovely little sloop. In the winter of 1973 he used the rebuilt *Dictator* as a plug and produced three very fast thirty-one-foot sloops. Also Bruno & Stillman in Newington, New Hampshire, built a thirty-foot model which has pleased many owners.

So with our jury-rigged bowsprit and the Society burgee at the masthead, we slipped by Garrison Island and joined the fleet.

31 Grounding Out

Eastward sails a long season. She goes overboard with a coat of topside and bottom paint in early May and is hauled for the winter in late November. In order to bring her through with a reasonably clean bottom, we ground her out in July, clean her off, and slap on another coat of bottom paint. Could there be a better time to do it than just before the race?

With high water about seven a.m., we slipped alongside a wharf over a hard gravel bottom, ran out spring lines and breast lines to hold *Eastward* in position against the pilings, and had breakfast as the tide ebbed. Presently she grounded with the gentlest of bumps. At once she felt awkward, too stable, her stern a little too high.

When she was solidly aground, we ran the throat halyard out to a strap around a beam in the wharf and hove taut to give the vessel a decided list.

We cleaned up the dishes. Harold and I swung our legs over the edge of the wharf and watched the tide go. The curious gathered about. Suburbanites on vacation strolled down to see the sailboat; they walked *so* slowly, swinging their cameras hung round their necks *so* slowly from side to side. They are shy, these visitors, completely out of their element, curious, yet not wanting to appear conspicuous. They have nowhere to go and all morning to get there,

Eastward *grounded out at Friendship.   Howard Taylor is cutting in the waterline.*

so they stroll.   Mary and I were in Nassau once, strolling along the wall where the native conch sloops tie up.   We liked it there.   We were in no hurry.   Mary raised the camera to take a picture of a man opening conches on the deck of a sloop.   He looked at us, dropped his knife, dove down the hatch, reappeared with a camera and took our picture.   Served us right.   We all laughed.

Then Mr. Murphy came briskly down the wharf.   He had been to see Murray Peterson and had from him a set of *Eastward*'s plans.   In his backyard in Swampscott, he had a new *Eastward* set up and was curious about construction details.   We poked in under the cockpit seats and discussed the horn timber and rudder port. Robert Gardner, another amateur builder, his sloop almost finished, joined the clinic. The tide dropped some more.   The beach under the bow was bare.

Howard Taylor, my brother-in-law and mainsheet man in many earlier races, appeared with old clothes, a heavy long-handled scrub brush and my boots.   I went over to Al Roberts's wharf and bought a bucket of "superclorox."

By now the tide was down so we could walk around the bow. We dismantled the jury-rigged bobstay, sprung a new thimble into

Working on the broken bobstay shackle. The jibstay and
topmast forestay have been cast off. (Prenatt)

Another view of Eastward *grounded out. (Prenatt)*

the wire splice, fitted a new shackle and put it all back together. The tide dropped farther. Tipping the brush into the bucket, I went to scrubbing while everyone else passed helpful hints and good advice.

There weren't any real weeds on her, just a slippery green slime. The clorox and brush took it right off. Behind me came Bob with buckets of clean rinsewater. Before my back got too tired, I Tom-Sawyered some one else into taking a turn on the brush so by the time the tide was below the rudder, *Eastward* was pretty well cleaned off and drying in the hot sun.

We ate lunch under a tree where all morning my sister had been reading a book. She treated us to sandwiches, gingerale, and a carefully-considered and heart-felt lecture on the futility and immorality of the Puritan work ethic. Still smelling of superclorox and mud, we were hard to convince.

The tide stopped going out. *Eastward* lay against the pilings, awkwardly balanced on her keel with her stern cocked up, her bottom drying, her decks cluttered with gear and stained with mud. The tide began to come.

We left the shade of the green tree for the work ethic. We mixed paint. Copper paint — fisherman's copper anyway — must be thoroughly mixed and then poured vigorously from pail to pail, "boxed," to get the poisons well acquainted with each other. It is a soft, flat paint, slopped on liberally with wide brushes. It must not be allowed to dry hard before the water covers it. Thus it stays soft so any weed or barnacle that sits down on it is poisoned first and then sloughed off, taking a bit of the surface with him. Howard, being the tallest, cut in the waterline. A fisherman, temporarily at leisure, came down on the beach to inspect the scene. He watched Howard carefully take up a brushful of paint and gingerly cut the red line up to the white topside.

"The way to do that," he said, "is to take a good confidence drink and then just walk right around her."

As we painted, the tide crept up to the keel, wet the after end of it, and ripple by ripple moved up the beach. We painted steadily ahead of it and by the time we finished off at the bow, our feet were wet. I did most of the painting in under the turn of the bilge aft where I had to paint almost over my head and the paint ran stickily down the brush handle. I pulled my hat way over my eyes and had a care and was very careful. One year I got a drop of copper paint in the eye. It hurt something frightful. My friend the doctor averred that no doubt the paint had irritating oils in it. I had suddenly become an eminent authority on irritating oils and wanted none of my crew to get the treatment. The doc gave me some castor oil to put in it and it helped some.

The tide kept coming. John Gould, who wrote *Farmer Takes a Wife, Last One In, The Fastest Hound Dog in the State of Maine,* and other distinguished literary works, walked up with his wife, Dottie. Was there anything we needed?

Oh yes, a bath! While the tide crept up toward the propeller shaft, we had hot baths with lots of soap and returned, clean and relaxed, to find the water slopping under the counter and the bow afloat. We cast off the throat halyard, singled up lines, took in fenders, and, no longer afraid to walk on the side away from the wharf, made ready to leave. She lifted, bumped and lifted again. Harold took a steady strain on the stern line. The next time she lifted, she slid back a foot and then very quietly slid off, afloat again, alive again, clean and smooth on the bottom.

We went off and anchored and spent an hour washing decks, coiling down lines, stowing fenders and generally cleaning up. Nothing makes a boat so dirty as grounding out.

All afternoon sloops had been coming in, running up the harbor from the westward, or slipping through Garrison Island passage from the east. Most were recognized as soon as the mainsail rounded the point. The saluting cannon barked. The helmsman, sitting relaxed on the wheelbox, waved. Daughters, well sunned, arose from the top of the cabin house. A son stood by forward. Friends already anchored hailed and were answered. The skipper picked out a spot, rounded to. Son forward dropped jib and staysail. As she lost way, the anchor was eased over, the mainsail lowered, and there she sat, unmistakably a Friendship with her wings tucked up like a tern.

Above: *Gloucester fisherman* Adventure *carrying passengers up Friendship Harbor the day before the race. In the foreground is the sloop* Depression. *Below: A wharf at Friendship with part of the fleet beyond. Note the lapstrake peapod alongside the float. (Both photos by Prenatt)*

One after another, all evening, sloops dropped in until there was scarcely swinging room for another. Riding lights flickered a little. Outboards churned. The click of oarlocks, the *psst* of opened beer cans, the murmur of quiet conversation gradually died away and the fleet lay under the stars to the ripple of the ebb tide.

32 Before the Race

The dedicated yacht racing skipper is a formidable character. He knows that to win he must leave nothing undone. He "tunes" his boat, and he does not mean it metaphorically either. He takes up a half a turn on this turnbuckle, slacks off a quarter turn on that one, measures the tension of the headstay with a gauge and takes up on the permanent backstay, as one ocean-racing man told me, "till the lifelines go slack." If his mainsail seems a mite too full just above the tack, he will send it back to the sailmaker to be re-cut. If his jib flutters on the leach, he will use it for a winter cover for the skiff and order a new one. Ballast must be adjusted ever so little this way and that. On a windy day he wears three heavy sweaters and jumps overboard before the race to take on water ballast. There is no end to his ingenuity.

A Friendship sloop owner, though, is by nature a different sort of person. He likes to go sailing and to get the best out of his boat, but he will make neither the boat nor himself uncomfortable to do it. A Friendship needs a little slack in her lee shrouds. Going to windward she wants a good mouthful of wind. She will get there faster sailing four and a half points off the wind with the end of the boom over the quarter and a full mainsail than she will with the sheet blocked right down hard and the luff a-shiver. The headstays are always a bit slack on a Friendship because there can be no permanent backstay and although the old-time skipper sprung his mast and topmast forward a bit to tighten the luff of the jib and the leach of the main, tuning *is* a metaphorical expression in Friendships. We are ordinarily a pretty relaxed crowd.

However, on the morning of the race, a change is evident. Here is a man aloft in a bosun's chair figuring a way to raise his staysail halyard block six inches. Over yonder two men are setting up lanyards with a little watch tackle. It is impossible to get a three-eighth-inch stainless steel wire shroud singing taut in a Friendship sloop by this or any other means but they are trying their best.

At nine-thirty a skipper's meeting is called. Skiffs begin to congregate at the ladders of Al Roberts's wharf. Keep off the float! Lobstermen are buying gas and bait or landing lobsters, for it is business as usual with them. The skipper who comes late must climb over half a dozen skiffs, prams, punts, dories and peapods to get to the ladder, and the mess of painters at the top makes the Gordian knot look like a bowline.

Skippers, friends, crews, interested onlookers, children and dogs gather around when Bill Danforth appears at the head of the stairs leading to the second floor of the building on the wharf. John Gould, about to make a dump run, pauses in his loaded truck. Bill's big black dog, Pat, stands beside him as Bill tells us that the weather report sounds favorable, that we will start at twelve, and that some skippers have been confused about port and starboard tack. "If your sail is on the port side," says Bill, "you're on the starboard tack and have the right of way." Questions on more complex aspects of the racing rules are explained in careful and accurate detail but are clearly not comprehended by a fair percentage of those present. The principle that at Friendship we are all friendly and no one should run into anyone else or lodge a protest seems to cover most of the rules.

Someone asks for a clock check so he will know precisely when to expect the ten-minute gun. Bill consults his official timepiece.

"In ten seconds it will be exactly nine-forty, nine, eight, seven . . ." Pat begins to whine and tries to get down the stairs past Bill. ". . .

five, four, three . . ." Pat bolts for the door behind him but brings up short on his leash. ". . . two . . . one . . . MARK." Pat jumps up to lick Bill's face and thank him. He hates guns, and whenever he hears a countdown, he anticipates gunfire. When it doesn't come, he is effusively grateful.

Betty Roberts circulates, collecting for banquet tickets, passing telephone messages, answering questions. John Gould leaves for the dump, and a bait truck loaded with the carcasses of redfish from the Rockland freezing plant backs onto the wharf with Al in the back flourishing a two-tined fish fork. He looks harrassed, and with good reason for everyone wants everything right away five minutes ago.

We leave the mob on the wharf and return to *Eastward*, where Mary has been making sandwiches for a regiment. We have Howard, Bob, Harold, Mary and the skipper to race the boat.

Aboard *Eastward*, there is no tension. We are an easy and relaxed crew. The skipper is no Captain Bligh. To be sure, we have set up the rigging as tight as we can get it, taped the jib snaps closed so they can't catch the jib topsail sheets, lined up the two-bladed propeller vertically behind the deadwood, pumped out all the bilgewater we can extract. Two of the deck boxes in the cockpit we have put aboard the peapod, which will be tied to the anchor line and left in the harbor. With the boxes out, there is less weight aft and more room to handle sheets. The small anchor, boarding ladder, fender board, inflatable life raft, and other excess gear is stowed in the peapod, too, in order to save weight and clear the decks. But there is no tension.

Howard lashes our racing numbers in the rigging. We set the mainsail, Bob and Harold on the halyards get the throat up, then the peak.

"Up a hair more," I tell Harold, who is holding a turn on the pin and swaying on the halyard a mite. "Just a grind more. I want a little wrinkle from the peak down toward the tack." The blocks squeak and are still. Reef points tap in the light air. The sheet hangs slack.

The foredeck hands coil down halyards, swinging their arms to make big coils. Then they dump the topsail out of its bag on the foredeck, bend on halyard, sheet and jackstay.

"Did you remember to oil the snap shackles?" asks Bob, innocently. One year we started a race from anchor, the slower boats starting first. With a premium on speed in setting sails and getting under way, we oiled the snap shackles on the topsail sheet and halyard. When our signal was hoisted, the crew swarmed on deck, cast off stops, set the mainsail and hauled the anchor simultaneously and with furious haste. Staysail and jib sizzled up the stays. The topsail was bent and started aloft; but as it climbed above the lee of the mainsail, and slatted in the wind, the snap shackle on the halyard unsnapped from the head of the sail. Bob swarmed up the mast using halyards, mast hoops, anything that would support hand or foot. He stood on the spreaders, embraced the topmast, and grabbed the swinging wire halyard. He snapped it to the sail and passed a mousing to prevent it from slatting loose again.

Up went the sail, but before it could be sheeted home, the sheet unsnapped from the clew and ran out to the cheek block at the peak of the gaff.

"Shall I go get it?" called Bob from the spreader.

"No!" shouted his mother and I together. Surely, we felt, it would be better to take the time to lower the mainsail and retrieve the sheet from the peak of the gaff than for our son to risk the perilous trip to the upper tip of the spar. "No!" we shouted.

While we watched, he stepped off the spreader on to the gaff, seized the peak halyards for support, scuttled up the steeply-sloped spar like a squirrel, and returned with the sheet between his teeth. He snapped it to the clew of the sail, moused it, and was on deck before the sail was full.

"It was O.K.," he said. "The sail was out over the water." We have never oiled snap shackles since that day.

33 The Start

With an hour to ge before the first gun, we set the topsail, found a wrinkle across it, lowered the peak and then the throat, set the peak up taut again and accepted it. We slipped the anchor line, leaving the skiff grotesquely loaded, and beat down the harbor toward the starting line. On the way, we set the jib topsail and practiced tacking ship.

"Ready about." Howard, on the stern, casts off the weather backstay tackle. Harold lets fly jib and jib topsail sheet, the latter, a single part of quarter-inch manila, snaps viciously.

"Hard a-lee." I roll the wheel over. *Eastward* swings purposefully into the wind, all sails a-luff. I seize the new weather backstay and pass it aft to Howard on the stern. While he is setting it up, Harold subdues the new lee jib topsail sheet while Mary catches a turn on the cleat. Bob on the foredeck handles the jib sheet. *Eastward* fills on the new tack, moves out. Harold takes the slack in the jib sheet from Bob. Bob calls the headsails: "Ease the kite (jib topsail) a whisker — No, take it in. Trim jib a grind." And we are off on the new tack. It is an intricate maneuver requiring training, teamwork, and muscle applied to the right places. We try it three or four times, improving each time. Still, no strain. We might be out for just a gentle morning sail. Bob takes in the kite. We will

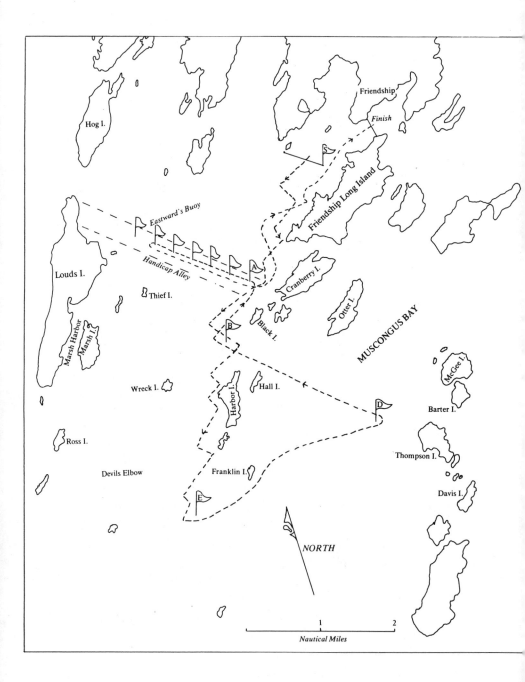

Friendship

Finish

Friendship Long Island

Eastward's Buoy

Handicap Alley

Louds I.

Thief I.

Marsh Harbor

Marsh I.

Cranberry I.

Black I.

Otter I.

MUSCONGUS BAY

McGee I.

Wreck I.

Harbor I.

Hall I.

Barter I.

Ross I.

Thompson I.

Devils Elbow

Franklin I.

Davis I.

E

NORTH

Hog I.

1   2

Nautical Miles

not need it until just before the start and really have not time to handle the extra sheets and backstays.

We slip by Bill Danforth's committee boat, *White Falcon*, read the course designation, tack again, and run down the starting line to see how the wind sits. To us, it seems to favor a port tack start on the windward end of the line. We try a trial run, heading away from the line while Mary calls off the seconds on the stopwatch. At one minute and thirty seconds we tack and head back for the buoy on the windward end of the line. At three minutes thirty-five seconds since we crossed the line, we cross it again, but we are too far to windward. A boat to leeward of us could force us above the mark. We try again. Still no strain aboard *Eastward*.

Other skippers are doing the same thing. As we head for the line on the port tack, the huge *Tannis*, nearly forty feet long with an acre of mainsail, comes rushing at us on the starboard tack. We bear off to leeward of her and find two little fiberglass twenty-four-footers ahead of us and Bill Pendleton's big *Blackjack* crowding them from their lee side. There is a narrow hole to go through; Bill eases off a bit to make room, someone shouts "Hold your course" and we slip by. Here comes Mal Barter in *Dirigo*, a Lash Brothers' sloop, running back to try the start, blowing his horn and shouting "Starboard" at a dumpy little black sloop astern. We watch the most dangerous opposition — Barter in *Dirigo*, Phil Cronin in *Rights of Man*, Jack Cronin in *Tannis*, and Gordon Winslow in *Channel Fever*. As the time for the ten-minute gun gets closer, we keep away from the weather end of the line and jog around looking as innocent as we can. So do they. But there is still no tension on *Eastward*, hardly.

Mary watches the committee boat, stopwatch in hand. "He's bending on the white flag . . . He's loading the cannon. There's Bill looking at his watch . . . I wish those boats would get out of the way. I can't see anything."

"Bump," goes the gun. "Click," goes the watch.

"Trim main sheet."

"Nine forty-five to go."

"Watch Barter coming up to leeward."

"I got him. Ready about."

"Nine-thirty to go."

Not much tension.

With eight twenty-five to go, we take a run away from the line, tack, and head back but not hard up to the buoy. Several sloops are up to windward, obviously going for the buoy, crowding each other, shouting. We come up toward the line going fast.

"Five forty-five to go."

"Flag down. Five thirty to go."

"Looks good, Cap," from the foredeck.

"Ease mainsheet. We're early."

"Watch the black one behind you."

"We got him. He's overtaking."

"Trim main."

"Bump," goes the gun.

"Too late."

"Watch Pendleton on starboard."

"O.K., ease main." We are well over the line now and it is time to tack back. "Ready about."

"Four thirty."

"In the main a bit."

"Watch that green one."

"Never mind him. We're on starboard."

"I don't think he knows it."

"Cut him in half! Starrr-board!"

"That gets him."

"Four minutes."

"What happened to four fifteen?"

"Never mind, I said four fifteen."

"Ease main, slack jib, we'll hang around the line awhile." *Eastward* slows, hangs in the wind close to the line.

"Three forty-five. Time to go. Trim main, trim jib."

"Three thirty." We are under way again on the starboard tack reaching away from the line for the spot we want, a spot from which we can tack and just make the buoy hard on the wind in two minutes and five seconds. Ahead of us a mob is bearing down on the port tack, headed for the line already. We find a hole in the phalanx as they crowd to clear us.

"Two fifteen."

"That was close."

"Two minutes."

"Ready about. Damn. No, we can't tack right in front of *Tannis*. Gybe - o. Slack mainsheet." *Eastward* turns sharply to leeward. The main slams over and *Tannis* tears by to windward, blanketing us momentarily.

"One forty-five." Cronin's crew, enough of them to man a privateer, laugh and wave. We have lost a little time, but not much.

"Trim main. Give her the kite."

The jib topsail whizzes up the stay.

"Kite sheet!" from Howard. Then sharply,

"Watch that topmast. Backstay. Backstay. Hurry up."

Howard sets up the backstay to support the topmast.

"One fifteen."

"One fifteen! We're late! Miles late! Look at all those guys ahead of us. We've had it!"

"They're all early. Sail the boat, Cap."

"In main."

"One minute."

"They *are* early. Look at them bear off. They're running down the line. That will kill Ted Brown." The whole mob barges downwind illegally on those heading up for the line. We are too busy to watch.

"Forty-five seconds."

"Watch Winslow to windward. He's coming down on you."

"He can't do that."

"He is."

"I can't bear off. Here's *Ellie T* to leeward, Pendleton just ahead of me and Phil Nichols in *Surprise* coming up astern."

"Thirty seconds, flag down."

I yell at Winslow, suggesting in vigorous language that he is barging on me and I have the right of way. But he is being crowded by another to windward of him, all of us trying to squeeze by the buoy. Here are half a dozen ten-ton boats, all moving at five knots and rushing together, all committed to squeezing to leeward of that little red flag. We bear off sharply, swinging our bowsprit over Pendleton's cockpit while Winslow's swings over ours. Phil Nichols somehow holds back so he hits neither us nor Winslow and slips to leeward. The one to windward of Winslow goes the wrong side of the mark as we come back on course.

"Bump," goes the gun.

There may have been some tension there for a minute, but we nothing was broken.

"We smell like roses!" shouted the foredeck hand. "In kite a grind."

There may have been some tension there for a minute, but we came out of the tangle on the crack of the gun to windward of the fleet and sailing fast. It was the best start we had seen in many a year.

34 The Finish

It was a grand sight. Nearly half a hundred Friendship sloops spread
out across Muscongus Bay leaning to a blue Maine southwester. One
of the best aspects of it was that they were all astern and to leeward.

Eastward is a hard boat to catch, but some of the newer ones had
learned something from watching the competition and they came on
strong. *Rights of Man* was coming up astern. *Channel Fever*, her
wind clear at last, was to leeward but working up on us and sailing
fast. The fleet began to spread out. *Hieronymus* came out of the
press to threaten for a while, moving fast with her new topsail.

"*Rights* is tacking."

"Let her tack. We'll hang on and try to cover Winslow."

"Better tack. Look at the fine draft *Rights* is getting under the
shore."

"Well, we aren't hurting Winslow much. Let him go. Ready
about." *Eastward* swung on her heel, sheets were loosed to starboard and gathered in to port. Harold swung on the jib topsail
sheet while Mary held on the cleat what he gained. The gear squeaked, stretched, and she settled down to work.

Because no two Friendship sloops are exactly alike, the Society's
official handicapper, Cyrus Hamlin, has adopted for the Friendship
sloop races an ingenious scheme called "distance handicapping" for

making the faster boats sail a greater distance than the slower ones. Thus we all start together and the first boat across the finish line is the winner without the necessity of figuring a corrected time.

About two miles after the start of the race, the fleet rounds Buoy A and reaches off at right angles to the course. Along this reach, known as Handicap Alley, is placed a succession of buoys, each with a flag of a distinctive color. Each sloop is assigned a flag commensurate with its potential speed as calculated by Mr. Hamlin's computer. After rounding her flag, each sloop returns to Buoy A and continues the race, running the alley again as she approaches the finish. A further refinement assigns winners a five percent extra handicap for each race won. Thus *Eastward*, a frequent winner, has piled up a handicap exceeded by only one other sloop. Consequently, although we were among the first around Buoy A, we were well back among the fleet when we emerged from the alley.

It had breezed up by the time we got down to Thompson's Island. A gybe around the mark looked like questionable policy. The mainsail and topsail together are huge, and if a backstay got caught, the topmast was as good as gone. However, we were in a boat race so we slammed her over. Nothing caught, nothing broke, no one got hurt so we were well out of it. *Rights* and *Channel Fever* were still ahead, and ahead of them were four or five others.

We ran the alley again, to the benefit of everyone but *Eastward*. On the run back into Friendship with *Hieronymus* and *Rights* now both ahead of us we tacked downwind so as to keep our headsails — all three of them — full on the starboard side and to head out into the bay. We had little to lose by the experiment for no one in our class was close to us. However, when we gybed and came in, we found Gordon Winslow in *Channel Fever*. We slipped across his bow, got in to windward of him, and bore off for the finish line so he would have to go through our lee. He was moving fast and slipped by, but we then maneuvered our mainsail over his cockpit so it blanketed his sail. We gained on him, but in order to pass him, we had to swing away from him, clearing his wind. We would surge ahead, but then he would pick up speed, and catch us. We blanketed him again, surged ahead again, and dropped back.

As we came up the shore of Friendship Island, the wind increased and worked westerly so as to put us by the lee, that is, with the wind on the port quarter and the sail on the port side. I didn't want to gybe on to the port tack, releasing his mainsail and giving him the right of way, but it would be difficult to cross the finish line without gybing.

The two of us rushed down on the line, first one ahead and then the other, both by the lee, both going better than six knots. Bill Danforth's boat marked our end of the line. I bore off more and more, the wind in my left ear now, trying not to gybe, trying to cover *Channel Fever*'s mainsail, trying to slip by the committee boat. Bob was holding the jib topsail winged out by its sheet. Mary held the staysail out with the boathook. The jib pulled to port with the draft off the staysail. Howard sat on the stern manipulating the mainsheet as the boom threatened to decapitate Winslow and then

Friendship sloops running up Muscongus Bay toward the finish of a race. Dirigo *on the far right is coming up fast. (Prenatt)*

to dismast his sloop. A hundred yards from the finish the seizing parted which held the strap on the upper backstay block. Suddenly we had no backstay. The topmast bent and whipped as the jib topsail yanked on it. Howard passed me the mainsheet, grabbed what he could of the backstay and held on.

We flashed by Winslow on one of our surges ahead, on the verge of a gybe which would have wiped Bill Danforth's race committee, cannon, superstructure and dog into Friendship Harbor together. We beat *Channel Fever* by one second, but the others were way ahead so we got no hardware.

There may have been a little tension there.

We took in the jib topsail, main topsail and jib, picked up our mooring, furled sails, and sat in the cockpit watching some very exciting finishes as half a dozen big sloops in a heap swooped down on the line, mainsails straining, each with a great bone in her teeth. *Tannis* lost her topmast in a puff under Hall's Island and *Eagle*, fouled by the end of *Voyager II*'s boom, parted a topmast shroud and lost the spar. It was a headlong rush up the harbor.

If Cy Hamlin, our handicapper, had done a perfect job, everyone would have sailed a distance in Handicap Alley to make up for differences in his boat's speed and skipper's skill such that all forty-nine entries would have finished simultaneously. He did not quite achieve that, but he came close enough to it to more than satisfy some of us.

35 Friendship Sloop Day

The next day was thick and the race was cancelled. Later in the day a wind breezed up and the fog lifted so we had a good sail. But of the final day of the 1973 races, Friendship Sloop Day, I have only vague and confused memories of imminent disaster, disappointing confrontations, and wretched conclusion.

It blew hard that Saturday from the southwest. The schedule called for a "Parade of Sloops." That is, the sloops were to sail by Al's wharf in succession while an announcer with a loudspeaker told the assembled multitude about the boat. Accordingly we beat up to windward and with no jib topsail set, swung down the wind for the wharf. *Tannis* and *Rights* were ahead of us and we had delayed so that there would be plenty of room between us.

Clarence Hale, our sailmaker, had joined us and my brother Donald was aboard with his bagpipes. He got up on the foredeck and unleashed the instrument while I tried to keep from gybing as we roared by the wharf at seven knots, a bit by the lee. The scene was cluttered with anchored boats, the tide was running briskly, little children in prams, outboards, and unhandy inflatable rafts paddled about. Sloops which had already passed the wharf were beating out and had the right of way over us. Donald, in a break between "Scotland the Brave" and "Cock of the North," gasped, "I'd never take my boat down in there."

191

I never heard a note he played. I never heard the announcer or the crowd on the wharf. We never scratched paint, but it was close as we crossed tacks with *Tannis* and *Rights* on the beat out.

The race was wild. It breezed up some more so we took in the main topsail to keep the lady on her feet. She sails faster that way. We tried for the weather end of the line on the starboard tack but were late, found a mob to windward of us, and *Eastward* got discouraged and wouldn't sail. Maybe we had the mainsheet too tight. Maybe I pinched her up too close to the wind. Maybe there was too much dirty air to windward. Maybe when everyone is up to hull speed as we were in that breeze, there is less difference between boats. No matter how badly one sails in that breeze, his boat will do nothing less than hull speed. Anyway, we were well back at the A mark, and after the handicaps we were out of contention for the hardware.

The wind eased in the later part of the race and we had another close finish, this time with *Dirigo*. A fast boat before the wind, she caught us on the run home, and we blanketed her just as we had blanketed *Channel Fever*. However, when we crossed the line, she was a second ahead.

The race was won by *Dictator*, a thirty-one-foot sloop built by Robert McClain in 1915 and rebuilt by Jarvis Newman just in time for the race. He replaced almost every timber and plank in her and came out with a beautifully shaped hull, a big rig, and a modest handicap. In the winter of 1973-74, he used her as a plug to make several fiberglass hulls — the family is hard to beat. As *Dictator* swept across the finish line, she executed some sort of wild Chinese gybe — we were not there to see it — and caught her gaff bridle over the top of her mast, posing an engineering problem which kept the victor out of circulation for a while.

Having finished seventeenth among the replicas, the lowest *Eastward* had ever been, we picked up our mooring rather quietly. However, our spirits were soon revived by my brother on the pipes. Ribbons flying in the wind, he paced the foredeck and skirled to the immense satisfaction of the whole fleet. Each rendition was followed by shouts of "more, more," loud whistles and cannonfire. That night at the banquet he was elected by acclamation official piper to the Friendship Sloop Society.

And we remembered the story of the whaling skipper in the dying years of the whaling trade who sailed the seas and oceans of the world for four long years without killing a whale. He froze in the icy blasts of the Bering Sea and saw the pitch bubble from the deck seams on the Line, and he came home at last with a dry ship. His neighbors were sympathetic, so sympathetic that at last he lost patience.

"Yes," he said, "we went four years and we never got a barrel of oil, but, by God, we had one hell of a fine sail!"

Skiffs thronged alongside, our cockpit overflowed with visitors onto the decks and the top of the house. A klatch of teenagers held the foredeck, and joy was unconfined.

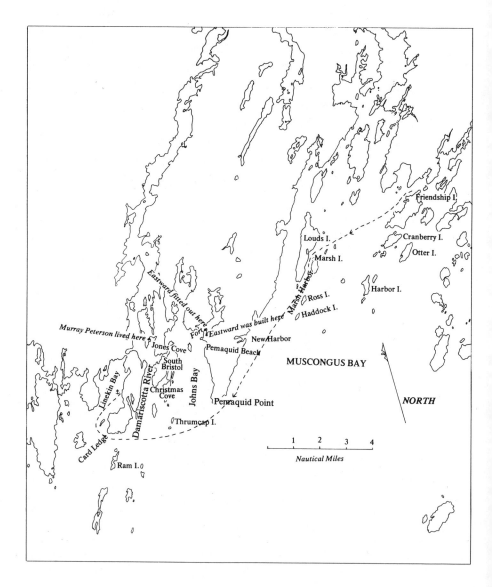

Friendship I.

Cranberry I.

Otter I.

Louds I.

Marsh I.

Harbor I.

Eastward fitted out here

Ross I.

Haddock I.

Murray Peterson lived here

Fort

Eastward was built here

New Harbor

Jones Cove

Pemaquid Beach

MUSCONGUS BAY

South
Bristol

Linekin Bay

Damariscotta River

Christmas
Cove

Johns Bay

Pemaquid Point

NORTH

Card Ledge

Thrumcap I.

| 1 | 2 | 3 | 4 |

Nautical Miles

Ram I.

36   Homeward Bound

All good things come to an end, and the good weather ended with the races. Sunday morning was thick, overcast, and stark calm. The fog lay heavily and still, dripping from the rigging. We knew we had to go home to Boothbay and we approached the day slowly, taking a relaxed breakfast, an extra pot of coffee and a half hour of good conversation. But at last we had to face it.

Mary and I rowed ashore to say good-bye to Al and Betty Roberts and to thank them for their generous efforts in organizing and carrying out the regatta. On the wharf were other skippers, standing around, kicking the pilings meditatively, wondering whether to start out or not. One heard we were going to Boothbay and asked if he could follow us. Another spoke up. And before we pushed off we had agreed to convoy five other sloops, ranging in size from one as big as we were to Frank Perkins's *Departure*, only fifteen feet long. The speed of the convoy was to be three knots.

We started off in fog so thick that we could see only our next boat astern and had to pass the word back to see that we were closed up. By clock, compass and fathometer we strolled down the shore of Friendship Island, across Handicap Alley to Thief Island, and on down Marsh Harbor. The fog scaled up and the breeze came in southwest outside Marsh Island so we set sail and turned the convoy loose to go their own ways. Some motored on; some sailed.

The twenty-four foot Angelus *in a trough off Pemaquid Point.*
She's bound for the Cape Cod Canal. (Prenatt)

Off New Harbor the wind fell light and a big lump of sea was running with loose floppy crests that occasionally fell over. We got to thinking, when we went down on a trough and could see only the peak of a mainsail where a sloop had been, that if one of those seas fell over on *Departure*, we might possibly be of some use. So we fired up the engine and chugged along, keeping her in sight. Off Pemaquid, *Angelus*, a wee twenty-four-footer, stood offshore in the gray afternoon headed for the Cape Cod Canal. The rest of us turned west for Boothbay.

As we crossed John's Bay, we could see up into Pemaquid Harbor where *Eastward* was built and we remembered her first sail on just such a lumpy gray day with a cool southeasterly blowing.

For three days we had been lying alongside the wharf off the Pemaquid Fort, fitting out. We had stowed ballast, Howard passing it down off the wharf to us; the boys, twins fourteen and John, eleven, carrying the smaller pieces. We stepped the mast with the "h'ister" on the wharf, remembering just in time to slip the mast hoops over the heel of it. We seized up the lower ends of the rigging around the deadeyes and set up manila lanyards as tightly as we could. We lost the forestay overboard, had to buy a grapple and drag for it and got it, to our delight and surprise. We put cleats and fairleads in the deck. I shinned up the mast with a shackle in my teeth and a block on my belt, shackled it into an eye and then was hoisted aloft in a bosun's chair like a gentleman. We hung blocks, spliced in running rigging, and finally on the third day under a lowery sky bent sails. We nearly had a boat.

I lifted the hatch to look at the engine, an ancient Gray 4-22 with a magneto. The crankcase was full of a mixture of oil and water. I lowered the hatch gently and decided not to think about the engine for the time being. We would sail her to Boothbay, of course. With a fair easterly, the only problem was getting away from the wharf where we lay.

Eastward lay stern to the tide with the wind pushing her against the wharf. I took an anchor out in a skiff and dropped it halfway between the wharf and Beaver Island. Then we cast off from the wharf and she swung off to the anchor, lying head to wind and tide. With my heart in my mouth, I stood to the mainsheet while my brother set the mainsail.

It was enormous. I had sailed bigger vessels but never one with a mainsail bigger than this. It flapped and thrashed in the cold wind and finally settled down to a reasonable pattering as the peak came up. I wondered what would happen when that anchor came off the bottom.

Here was a brand new boat. She had been skillfully designed by an experienced and successful designer. She looked just right. She ought to sail well. But no one had ever sailed her before. She was pure theory expressed in wood and iron, rope and canvas. Suppose the theory was wrong? Suppose that huge mainsail laid her on her ear and she dragged ignominiously to leeward with her boom in the water. Suppose it held her in the wind so that even with the staysail she would not pay off and sagged ashore on her maiden voyage. Suppose we hadn't rigged her right and something slipped or parted as soon as the sail filled.

I couldn't stand and suppose any longer. Halyards were coiled. Murray Peterson, the designer; Jimmy Chadwick, the builder; and all their wives and children and a good number of local people who had watched her grow in Jimmy's shed — all were standing expectantly on the wharf. Donald held the anchor line in his hand.

"Get the anchor, Don," I said, "but don't lose it. We may need it again." Donald pulled steadily and *Eastward* surged ahead against the tide.

"Anchor's clear."

"Give her the staysail." Someone must have set the staysail. I slacked the mainsheet, pulled the staysail taut, and waited to see what would happen.

Eastward paused a minute, hanging in the wind, hesitant to take her first step; then the staysail filled and she swung off on her heel as if she did it every day. The mainsail filled, and she ran down the harbor. I felt at once that she was right. She had a solid "big-boat" feel about her. She wasn't bouncy but she settled herself down into the Atlantic Ocean, took the first little chop steadily and trampled it under foot without a pause. Outside, she went about her work confidently, rising to the seas, shouldering through the tops, and settling smoothly into the troughs, never breaking her stride.

By the time I thought to look back, Murray and Jimmy were scarcely distinguishable on the wharf but they knew and I knew that we had among us created something of beauty, power and grace.

We rounded Thrumcap, crossed the Damariscotta River, and passed the Hypocrites bell from which we had taken departure for Nova Scotia four weeks before. Ram Island lay ahead through the haze looking just as it always did on an afternoon sail. With sheets started, we made Card Ledge and Negro Island. In the smooth water of Linekin Bay we slipped up to our mooring and made fast.

Somehow, there should have been a fanfare. We should have felt

Right: *Snugging down on the home mooring. (T. Gray)*

triumphant on our return from distant lands. We should have felt regretful that it was all over. Instead, we just came in the way we always did, rowed ashore, and walked up the bank into the life we had left four weeks ago.

But it was a richer life than it had been before. We had failed, it is true, to reach the eastern shore of the Bay of Fundy; but we had had that night at sea, tearing through the fog and dark in a green glow of phosphorescence, to be wondered at by shearwaters at dawn. We had looked down from the top of Dorr Mountain on Mt. Desert and up at the cliffs of Grand Manan. We had seen the sun rise over a black sea a-sparkle, saved our swamped peapod, and like a doll at a beer party, cowered in the great docks of Saint John. We had smelled the smokehouses of Seal Cove, laughed at a black-back teasing a shag, and sailed two high-tension races. We who came home looked out on wider horizons than we who left, outward bound. We cannot lose what we gained that summer, for it will always be part of us and we will always have that share in each other.

Appendix

Eastward was designed with a specific purpose in mind: to be an efficient party boat. We chose a fishing boat model because a boat designed for fishing has most of the characteristics needed in a party boat. A fisherman wants a dry and stable platform from which to work. His boat must be handy enough to get him out and home again, and seaworthy enough to go to sea in anything but a real gale.

Murray Peterson adapted the design of the Friendship sloop to our purposes, keeping her salient features. *Eastward* has the handsome clipper bow of the old-timers and the low waist and flat run. Where most of the Friendship sloops have a hollow waterline, however, *Eastward* has a straight, wedge-shaped entrance. Thus she avoids the heavy shoulders which in a short boat result from the reverse curve in the bow coming out and then having to turn sharply in toward the stern. The bow sections below the waterline are also wedge-shaped but flare sharply above it in order to keep the deck dry and to provide generous working space on the foredeck as well as buoyancy in the bow when running before the wind under a press of sail.

Eastward is a little deeper than the traditional Friendship sloop and, with a ton and a quarter of iron under her, is quite stiff. She carries about two tons of lead and iron in the bilge. When she was first built, her inside ballast was all iron. However, steel shafting

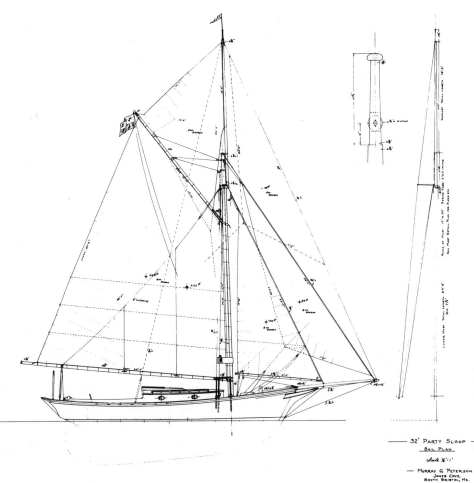

32' PARTY SLOOP
SAIL PLAN

Scale ⅜" = 1'

— MURRAY G. PETERSON —
JONES COVE
SOUTH BRISTOL, ME.

DESIGN No. 164   FEB. 7, 19

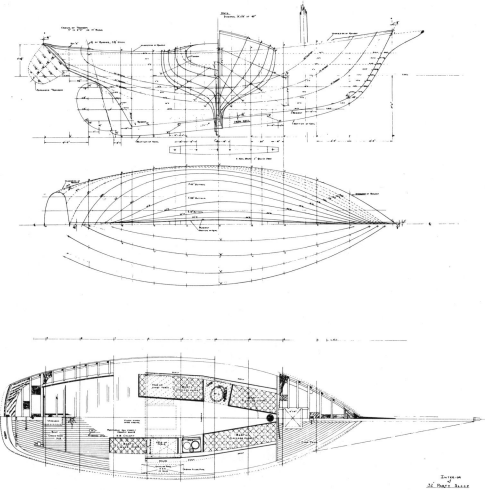

Interior
of
32' Party Sloop

and streetcar rails not only seriously affected the compass but occasionally changed their magnetic qualities so no compass compensation could be relied on. Therefore we bought junk lead, melted it, and poured it into bread tins to make eighteen-pound pigs which are clean, compact, and non-magnetic.

Eastward's stern is quite unlike the usual Friendship's stern. It is tucked up more like that of a Gloucester fishing schooner. At less than six knots, her run is flat and clean.

A heavy oak rub-rail and solid bitts — one forward and one on each quarter — are provided for frequent lying alongside floats and wharves. The bitts go down through the deck and are mortised into timbers below. We never use cleats to make fast to a wharf.

The cockpit, originally three feet longer than is shown on the plan, was designed to accommodate a maximum of ten passengers and for two years did so very successfully. On each side of the cockpit were lashed two boxes wide enough to sit on and as deep as the width of the widest board I could find, about twelve inches. They are used for life preservers, tools, and general stowage. About 1958 the Coast Guard imposed regulations on party boats carrying over six passengers, requiring watertight, gas-tight bulkheads, a powerful radio, a lifeboat on deck, and iron pipe rails, among other things. Consequently we decided to carry only six passengers, extended the house three feet aft and expanded the cuddy into a cabin.

The cockpit is supposed to be self-bailing, its floor about two inches above the level of the water outside. However, although the scupper hoses are crossed, the moment *Eastward* heels, water runs in through the scuppers into the lee corners of the cockpit. Even with the boat lying at anchor on an even keel, water will not run out because the cockpit floor pitches very slightly aft. We have installed sea-cocks on the scuppers, keep them closed most of the time and bail the cockpit.

The engine is under a big hatch in the cockpit floor. With hatch cover off, the engine is easily accessible and is open to light and air. The hatch is hinged athwartship so that the after half can be raised to start and ventilate the machine without exposing the engine itself to rain and spray. The engine is a forty-five-horsepower, four-cylinder Universal Flexifour. The exhaust runs hot from the engine to the muffler under the starboard side deck where cooling water is introduced through a hose from the block. As the engine is entirely below the waterline, there is an opening in the exhaust line to prevent water getting back into the manifold when the vessel is heeled to starboard in rough weather.

The engine turns an eight by seventeen-and-a-half two-bladed wheel on a one-and-a-quarter-inch bronze shaft. At 1100 r.p.m. it will drive *Eastward* at five knots; no engine will drive her much faster. Higher speed simply squats the stern down and drives water up the rudder post. In an effort to save money, I decided on a wooden rudder post working in an open trunk. It was a poor move. Not only does water overflow the top of it at times, but the seam between the rudder trunk and the horn timber cannot be reached to be caulked. She leaked quite badly here until we lined the rudder post with a bronze tube. The rudder should have had a bronze post working through a stuffing box as Murray Peterson originally advised.

Eastward's rig is big, simple, and unduly heavy. Maine summers can be gentle, day after day. Consequently we carry a big mainsail of nearly five hundred square feet, with staysail and jib of over one hundred square feet each. The topsail and jib topsail add over two hundred square feet more. It has to be a gentle day indeed when we can't move under sail. In winds up to about twelve knots, we carry full sail. The jib topsail, pulling directly on the top of the topmast which ordinarily has almost no support from aft, requires temporary running backstays. These are set up to the quarter bitts with a watch tackle on a three-sixteenth-inch stainless steel wire to the topmast head. We have lost two topmasts, both as the result of the mainsail's coming over against the taut backstay.

Without the jib topsail, *Eastward* will carry her main topsail comfortably and efficiently in winds up to about twenty knots, although it does not help very much sailing hard on the wind in a strong breeze. The gaff sags to leeward and luffs the topsail. One guest called it a "turbulator."

Under three lowers, the rig is efficient up to about twenty-five knots, but when *Eastward* buries her rail consistently, she slows down and sags to leeward. At that point, if we have not far to go, we take in the jib. However, this gives her a heavy weather helm and she is better with reefed mainsail and full jib.

The next shortening step is to take in the jib. She balances well enough under thirty-five knots with this dress if the sea is not too rough. Then the main can be double reefed and she will still go. If that sail is too much for her, it is high time to seek shelter.

Eastward heaves-to very well under staysail sheeted down hard and with the wheel turned hard to weather. Lying this way, the mainsail can be lowered and reefed, or it can be left standing with a slack sheet.

We have found the gaff rig has many advantages. On any point of sailing, except hard on the wind, a well-cut gaff sail with a fairly high peak is about as efficient an airfoil as a Bermuda sail. The top of it, stiffened and extended by the gaff, has less tendency to sag to leeward than the very narrow peak of a Bermuda sail. Also the center of effort is lower so there is less heeling moment for the same area. Off the wind the lower sail seems to have some advantage, too. The peak can be slacked a bit to bag the middle of the sail or sweated up to flatten it. In a squall, the peak can be slacked right off and the effective sail reduced by half in seconds. When the sail has to come down quickly, the weight of the gaff drags it down whether the boat is head to wind or not, for the hoops do not bind like slides on a track. Finally, the mainsail and topsail combined give more sail up high, set at a better angle, than the Bermuda sail.

In competition with really efficient modern vessels, *Eastward* cannot do well on the wind. With sheets started, however, she does very well indeed and has surprised a few of the yachting fraternity.

The shrouds supporting a comparatively short and heavy mast are three-eighth-inch stainless steel set up with deadeyes. We chose deadeyes because the sloop whose gear we planned to use in *Eastward* had deadeyes and even when we found her rigging would not do, we stayed with the plan. Certainly turnbuckles can set rigging tighter, but with a watch tackle, lanyards can be pulled tight enough to support the mast with just a little slack in the lee shrouds. The topmast shrouds are one-quarter-inch stainless steel and the head-stays, working from forward, aft are one-quarter-inch, five-sixteenth-inch and seven-sixteenth-inch stainless. Whisker shrouds are one-quarter-inch and the bobstay is seven-sixteenth-inch. All this is much heavier than needed and very reassuring. All ends except those of the jibstay are spliced around thimbles and served.

Running rigging is dacron — three-eighth-inch for headsails and seven-sixteenth-inch for main. There really is no strain the sails could put on sheets and halyards which would approach the break-ing strain of these lines, but a line smaller than three-eighth-inch is very hard to hold. Seven-sixteenth-inch is much easier to pull on and the mainsheet, running through two double blocks, sometimes takes some pulling.

The topsail is set on a jackstay. Its head hoists on a wire halyard to a sheave through the topmast head. The luff has a wire luff rope, terminating in a thimble about two-thirds of the way down the sail. This is shackled to a dacron jackstay spliced around the topmast about three feet above the lower masthead. With the halyard pulled taut, the shackle is a few inches above the top of the jackstay. The lower end of the jackstay is tightened down hard with a small watch tackle, stretching tight the wire luff close along the topmast. The tack is then snugged down and the clew hauled out to the end of the gaff with the sheet. It is a simple and durable rig, easily set and taken in to windward of the mainsail.

Eastward is heavily built on a frame of New Brunswick gray oak. Her frames are one and three-quarter-inch square, steam bent and notched to the keel. The lower four planks are oak and the rest of the planking Philippine mahogany finished to one-inch. It proved to be less expensive to buy mahogany logs, all clear stock, and have them sawn to specification than to buy twice as much Maine pine as was needed and pay a man's time to pick out the clear stock. There is a floor timber at every frame. A heavy oak bilge clamp runs the length of her right in the turn of the bilge on either side and a deck clamp just under the deck. For about ten feet abreast the mast there is a shelf, and heavy knees brace the partners. Deck framing is heavy and is covered with one-inch pine. The mast steps on a heavy timber spanning several floors and the step itself is drained to avoid standing water at the heel of the mast.

The cabin layout is developed for cruising comfort. First, the boat is open all the way from stern to counter to give a feeling of space and to encourage ventilation. Under the forehatch the anchor lines are coiled, the seventy-five pound yachtsman's anchor lying on its coil with the thirty-five pound plow on top of it. This is the anchor we use ordinarily with a three-quarter-inch nylon line. Aft of the forehatch is a half bulkhead, coming just above the bilge clamp, so anyone kneeling on the head of the forward bunk can easily get at the anchor line. Aft of this bulkhead is a bunk on either side, each arranged with a shelf behind it so that one can sit on the bunk and lean back against the shelf comfortably. The table between the bunks has no legs. It is supported on the forward end by a frame nailed to the bunks. Two bolts hold the table solidly to the frame. The after end is supported by a bridle to the carline overhead. The table folds in the middle on a piano hinge screwed to the underside, so that it can be stowed under the shelf against the side of the boat.

The port bunk is about two inches higher than the starboard one, which made it possible to install the head under a hinged cover at the aft end of the bunk. The whole forward cabin can be closed off with a curtain aft of the forward bunks, so one can use the head with adequate space, ventilation and privacy.

Aft of the bunk on the starboard side is a zinc-lined alcove for the Shipmate stove. The stove burns briquets and warms the cabin very pleasantly on a cool, damp evening. Also it makes a fine steady heat and gives us the use of an oven. There is a shelf for dishes behind the stove.

Aft of the stove is a low, narrow quarter berth extending under the cockpit with two shelves over it for pots and pans and bulky galley stowage. Against the 'thwartships bulkhead is a cabinet four inches deep with shelves the right height for mugs, mason jars, and the usual supermarket containers. Instead of having doors, this cabinet is covered by a single piece of plywood hinged at the bottom. Let down, it rests on the rail at the edge of the stove space and provides a large counter for the cook.

A sixteen-gallon stainless-steel water tank is under the deck on the starboard side of the cockpit and feeds by gravity to a faucet near the galley. No pump is necessary.

On the port side, aft of the head, is a bunk extending just to the bulkhead. Against the bulkhead on this side is another plywood leaf which swings down to form a chart table. The radio, fathometer, and radio direction finder are on the shelf over this bunk and quickly accessible to the navigator. Also, it is unnecessary for him to pick up everything at mealtimes, for galley and navigator's departments are entirely separate.

Headroom is about five feet eight inches, enough for almost everyone in our family. I would rather have people duck once in a while than build up topsides and deckhouse into a clumsy contrivance.

The cabin is lighted by four kerosene lamps on gimbals, which provide plenty of light for ordinary purposes. A seat on either of the after bunks is close enough to a lamp for reading.

Refrigeration is provided by a portable insulated ice chest stowed just forward of the mast. This is useful for what must be kept really cold, but for beer, oleomargarine, and many things less perishable, the locker under the quarter berth affords storage against the planking. In northern waters the locker is cool enough.

With such simple living arrangements we find little need to run the engine simply to charge batteries. We have two six-volt batteries which can be used either separately or in parallel. Navigation lights can be run off one battery and the other saved for starting the engine. The radio operates on a twelve-volt battery stowed under the bunk just forward of the head. The radio is used very little. When the battery gets low, it can be taken ashore and recharged.

Thus we have accommodations for four people in reasonable comfort and some privacy. If it is necessary to take more people, three can sleep in the cockpit on air mattresses under a tarp stretched over the boom and one on the cabin floor. However, this form of accommodation is not recommended. It means cooking for more than

four and stowing duffel bags, sleeping bags, and oil clothes in incon-
venient places. Also, four people, we find, are enough to have living
within thirty-two feet of each other. Seldom do we cruise with
more. Two people, of course, can dwell in luxury and frequently
have done so.